FEMALE GENITAL MUTILATION

A Call for Global Action

NAHID TOUBIA

GN
484
T68
1993

Female Genital Mutilation:

...ceives a decorated cloth for her initiation which ...on. She uses it for the rest of her life as a ...d into a secret society. The designs encode ...moral precepts, decipherable only by the women ...most specialized custodians of esoteric knowledge.

A Call for Global Action

Contents

- 5   Introduction
- 9   What is Female Genital Mutilation (FGM)?
- 13   What are the Complications and Effects of FGM?
- 21   Where and to What Extent is FGM Practiced?
- 29   Who Performs FGM?
- 31   Is FGM a Religious Practice?
- 35   The Cultural Significance of FGM
- 39   FGM and Children's Rights
- 43   A Global Call to Action
  - 45   Legal Remedies
  - 46   Recommendations for Action
- 48   Bibliography

ILLUSTRATIONS
Cover: Elizabeth Catlett
  The Black Woman Speaks
Cover background, inside cover
and details throughout book:
  Resist-dye cloth, cotton,
  Bamana, Mali. Courtesy
  of The Metropolitan
  Museum of Art, The
  Michael C. Rockefeller
  Memorial Collection,
  Bequest of Nelson
  A. Rockefeller, 1979.
  (1979.206.190)
p. 10   Stephen Gilbert
p. 11   Ciba-Geigy
p. 24   Nahid Toubia
p. 34   Nahid Toubia
p. 11   Bert Oppenheim

PHOTOGRAPHERS
Kay Churmish, UN/World Bank:
p. 15   #148463
Louise Gubb, UN Photos:
p. 16   #155644, Sudan
p. 30   #155647, Sudan
Diana Hrisinko:
Inside back cover
International Women's Tribune:
p. 2   Kenya
John Isaac, UN Photos:
p. 4   #153726, Mali
p. 7   #156684, Ethiopia
p. 13   #153763, Mali
p. 18   #156504, Ethiopia
p. 23   #153445, Senegal
p. 27   #154716, Mali
p. 33   #153754, Senegal
p. 36   #154717, Mali
p. 39   #153731, Senegal
p. 41   #152237, Egypt
Kay Muldoon, UN photo:
p. 9   #153382, Mali
Nahid Toubia:
p. 11   Sudan
YN/AB, UN photo:
p. 40   #101584, Nigeria

DESIGNER
Karen Davidson, New York

PRINTER
Rasco Graphics

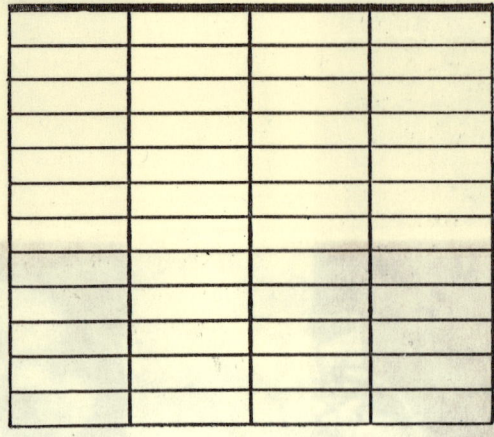

This second edition was funded
by UNICEF, New York and by
Population Action International.

**FOR COPIES OF
THIS PUBLICATION
CONTACT:**
Women, Ink.
777 United Nations Plaza
New York, NY 10017, USA
Tel: (212) 687-8633
Fax: (212) 661-2704

Published by RAINBO
All rights reserved.
Copyright © 1995.

Library of Congress Catalog Card
Number: 95-068983x

Acknowledgements

RAINB♀

Research Action Information Network for Bodily Integrity of Women is an international not-for-profit organization registered in New York State. Its mandate is to work on the intersection between health and human rights with particular attention to women's reproductive and sexual rights. In 1993 the Network launched its Global Action against FGM.

BOARD OF TRUSTEES

Abdullahi An-Na'im

Rev. David Ben Joseph

Chandra Bhudo

Lynn Freedman

Afaf Mahfouz

Jeff Mecaskey

Asha Samad

I would like to thank Jeff Mecaskey and Joanne Edgar of the Edna McConnell Clark Foundation for professional and personal support in the production of the first edition; Elizabeth Kirberger for her dedicated research and for assistance with the legal section; and Barry Ravitch for preparation of the maps.

Special thanks to the CIBA-Geigy Corporation; Stephen G. Gilbert and the Washington University Press; The United Nations Photo Library and the Metropolitan Museum of Art for permission to reproduce illustrations and art material; and the Museum of African Art, New York, for information on circumcision cloth.

Special thanks to Elizabeth Catlett, a powerful African-American artist, who made herself accessible and readily gave permission to use her artwork for the cover.

My deepest thanks and gratitude to Nanci Hersh, without whose constant support and encouragement this project would have never happened.

The most important acknowledgement must go to the brave African women and men who over the years spoke up against this practice, often at great personal sacrifice. This book would not have been possible without their work; I would not have the courage to continue without their example.

"All human beings are born free and equal in dignity and rights. They are endowed with reason and conscience and should act towards one another in a spirit of brotherhood [and sisterhood]."

—Article 1
Universal Declaration of Human Rights
(brackets added by author)

Introduction

Globally, at least 2 million girls a year are at risk of genital mutilation—approximately 6,000 per day.

An estimated 130 million girls and women in the world are genitally mutilated. *Most live in Africa, a few in Asia, and increasingly, there are more women in Europe, Canada, and the United States who have suffered female genital mutilation (FGM).*

These women and girls experience pain, trauma, and frequently, severe physical complications, such as bleeding, infections, or even death. Long-term physical complications are numerous, and there appear to be substantial psychological effects on women's self-image and sexual lives. For those with the severest form of FGM, infibulation, the trauma of mutilation is repeated with each childbirth.

Female genital mutilation—also commonly known as female circumcision—is an extreme example of efforts common to societies around the world to manipulate women's sexuality, ensure their subjugation and control their reproductive functions. In Western countries, for instance, women subject themselves to medically dangerous forms of cosmetic plastic surgery to increase their sexual desirability. Foot binding in China is another example.

Voices are being raised, both in Africa and abroad by women and men who want to eradicate FGM. This fight is not new. Courageous individuals and small groups of intellectuals were among the early African pioneers who dared to pierce the social sanctity surrounding FGM. Professional organizations, most often those of doctors and nurses, helped gather much of the information, particularly on health complications, now used to fight FGM. Today, many African and Asian communities are sifting through their cultures and revising some traditions, while holding on to others. The time is right for communities to rise up and protest female genital mutilation, without destroying their cultural integrity.

The attention of the world community on this issue has, so far, produced mixed results. When Western feminists in the 1970s and 1980s expressed their empathy by making public statements, undertaking studies, or pressing for national laws and international resolutions, they were extremely helpful in giving exposure to the issue and removing the shroud of silence which surrounded it. But others, particularly the less responsible elements of the popular press, mishandled the issue by sensationalizing it and treating African and Asian women in a condescending manner. Unfortunately, this crude approach to a complex issue has created a defensive reaction among many people involved with the practice who might otherwise be allies in the fight for eradication.

Recent efforts at the official international level, particularly by United Nations agencies, has successfully put FGM on women's health and human rights agendas. These groups see FGM as a health hazard and a form of violence against women. At the national level, many governments and national leaders have publicly denounced the practice, but few have translated their concern into laws prohibiting FGM or programs to persuade people to abandon it.

At the moment, there is a sense of bewilderment, both at the official level and among grassroots organizers, as to what can be done. The current high level of concern runs the risk of being reduced to indifference unless there is effective action. Women must not allow this to happen. In the past ten years, some initiatives were started in Africa that can be the basis for global action. The Inter-African Committee Against Traditional Practices Affecting the Health of Women and Children (IAC), was created by African women in 1984. It is now a nongovernmental organization (NGO) based in Geneva, with members in most countries where FGM occurs.

As African immigrants move throughout the world, taking FGM with them, many women are working to halt the practice in their new communities. Among the first organizations created by immigrant women to tackle this issue were The Foundation for Women's Health, Research, and Development and the Black Women's Health Action Project, both based in the United Kingdom and run by a few dedicated African women. They have been able to raise awareness and press for laws against FGM in Europe. They have also developed training material for health professionals and community action groups.

Effective programs such as these respect cultural integrity and work within the context of women's economic and social powerlessness. FGM must be understood within an economic and social framework; the financial value of marriage within traditional cultures and the ability of social and economic elites to define local custom are both key factors. FGM also has serious health implications, of course, but the effort to stop it must concentrate on individual and social identity and on changing women's consciousness. Even the human rights context, though crucial at the international level for passing resolutions and pressing governments to take action, is not appropriate for negotiating change at the family level.

At present, the weakest area of activity is at the national level, where programs must be organized on a scale large enough to bring about tangible results. After decades of debate, sporadic studies and random programming, it is time to take bigger steps. The rising movement against FGM among African women is proof that when women get rid of their psychological pain and fear they are able to cope with feelings that may have been buried for years. When they throw off the denial mechanisms they have used for survival, women are able to speak out and object to this inhuman and unnecessary suffering.

FGM involves women's many social roles: The practice relates to superstition, religion, local custom, health practices, childbearing, concepts of sexual fulfillment and a range of other important social relations. Changing attitudes towards FGM will inevitably involve change in the overall situation of women.

Women must not allow the continued marginalization of this issue. Although FGM cannot, and must not, be separated from other women's or social justice issues, it deserves attention in its own right. Funding levels for FGM programs must be similar to those for such high-profile programs as children's health, women's economic development, and family planning. **There is a pressing need for action that will draw on each country's mass communications systems and popular culture to disseminate information, generate internal discussion, and present the basic health and religious facts in an accessible manner.**

FGM is unnecessary. It is a violation of women's

right to preserve the integrity of their bodies.

FGM is an issue that concerns women and men who believe in equality, dignity and fairness to all human beings, regardless of gender, race, religion or ethnic identity. It must not be seen as the problem of any one group or culture, whether African, Muslim, or Christian. FGM is practiced by many cultures. It represents a human tragedy and must not be used to set Africans against non-Africans, one religious group against the other, or even women against men.

Our organization, RAINB♀, was started in June of 1994. It stands for Research, Action and Information Network for the Bodily Integrity of Women. Our purpose is to empower women all over the world to preserve their bodily integrity and their reproductive and sexual health and rights. We have launched the Global Action Against Female Genital Mutilation as a major project of our organizations.

This global action calls upon all peoples of all nations to come together in empathy, solidarity, and compassion, to create an environment where people feel safe to change their old ways without threat to their dignity, independence and cultural integrity.

"*The memory of their screams calling for mercy, gasping for breath, pleading that those parts of their bodies that it pleases God to give them be spared. I remember the fearful look in their eyes when I led them to the toilet, 'I want to, but I can't. Why Mum? Why did you let them do this to me?' Those words continue to haunt me. My blood runs cold whenever the memory comes back. It's now four years after the operation and my children still suffer from its effects. How long must I live with the pain that society imposed on me and my children?*"

—Testimony of Miami, from "Female Circumcision in Gambia," by Saffiatou K. Singhateh, in *Female Circumcision: Strategies to Bring About Change*, The Somali Women's Democratic Organization

What is Female Circumcision or Female Genital Mutilation?

Female genital mutilation or female circumcision is the collective name given to several different traditional practices that involve the cutting of female genitals. In this text FGM is not used to refer to minor forms of genital rituals, which may involve washing the tip of the clitoris, pricking it with a pin or separating and cleaning the foreskin (prepuce). The term FGM is reserved to describe ritualistic practices where actual cutting and removal of sexual organs takes place.

FGM is one of the traditional rituals that prepare girls for womanhood, although the age at which it is practiced varies widely. In some cultures, girls are circumcised as early as infancy, while in others, the ceremony may not occur until the girl is of marriageable age—approximately 14 to 16 years old. **Most commonly, girls experience FGM between four and twelve years of age, at a time when they can be made aware of the social role expected of them as women.**

In the communities where FGM takes place it is referred to as "female circumcision." This term, however, implies an analogy to male circumcision, which is not the case. Male circumcision is the cutting off of the foreskin from the tip of the penis without damaging the organ itself. The degree of cutting in female circumcision is anatomically much more extensive. The male equivalent of clitoridectomy (in which all or part of the clitoris is removed) would be the amputation of most of the penis. The male equivalent of infibulation (which involves not only clitoridectomy, but the removal or closing off of the sensitive tissue around the vagina) would be removal of all the penis, its roots of soft tissue, and part of the scrotal skin.

Despite the imprecision of the term female circumcision, it is used in this text as a recognition of the terms of reference of the communities where it occurs, and as a starting point from which to initiate the process of change.

Development of genitals in utero Showing the Correspondence Between Male and Female Genitalia

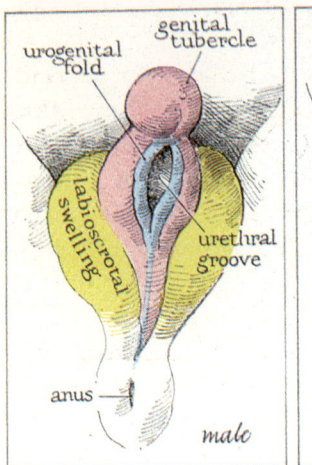
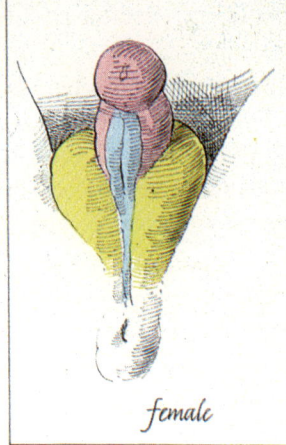

The external genitalia in the ninth week.

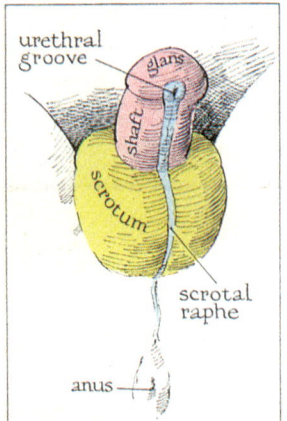
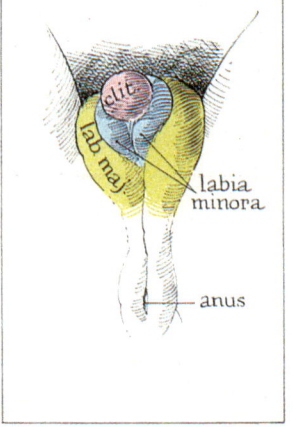

The external genitalia in the tenth week.

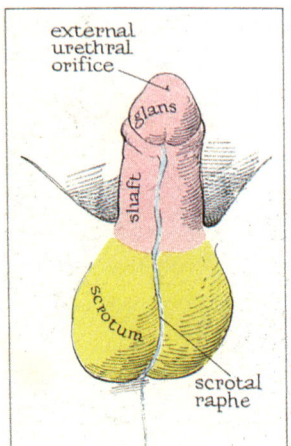
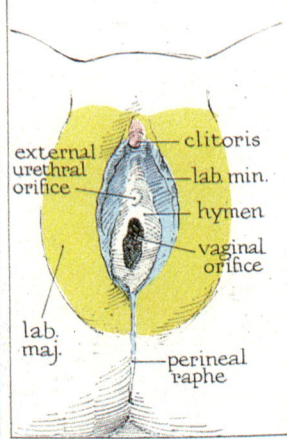

The external genitalia at term.

Types of Female Genital Mutilation

Although many studies refer to several different types of female genital mutilation, the different operations can be incorporated into three basic types:

Type I: *Clitoridectomy*

In this operation a part or the whole of the clitoris is amputated and the bleeding is stopped with pressure or a stitch. Careful review of the literature reveals no documented of a ritualistic circumcision where only the skin around the glans has been removed without damage to the sensitive part of the organ. It is this author's belief that male style female circumcisions are only done in modern surgical settings, usually on adult women.

Type II: *Excision*

Both the clitoris and the inner lips are amputated. Bleeding is usually stopped with stitching but the vagina is not covered.

Approximately 85 percent of all women who undergo FGM have either Type I or II.

Type III: *Infibulations*

In this group of operations, the clitoris is removed, some or all of the labia minora are cut off and incisions are made in the labia majora to create raw surfaces. These raw surfaces are either stitched together and/or kept in contact by tying the legs together until they heal as a "hood of skin," which covers the urethra and most of the vagina.

Since a physical barrier to intercourse has been created, a small opening must be reconstructed for the flow of urine and menstrual blood. It is surrounded by skin and tough scar tissue and is sometimes as small as the head of a match stick or the tip of the little finger. If the opening is more generous, sexual intercourse can take place after gradual dilation, which may take days, weeks, or even months. If the opening is too small to start the dilatation, **recutting has to take place before intercourse.**

Recutting also occurs with each childbirth to allow exit of the fetal head without tearing the tough tissue. After birth re-infibulation is performed where the raw edges are sutured again—often to the same size as existed before marriage, to recreate the illusion of virginal tightness. Because of the extent of both the initial and then repeated

Types of female genital mutilation (yellow areas indicate tissue to be removed)

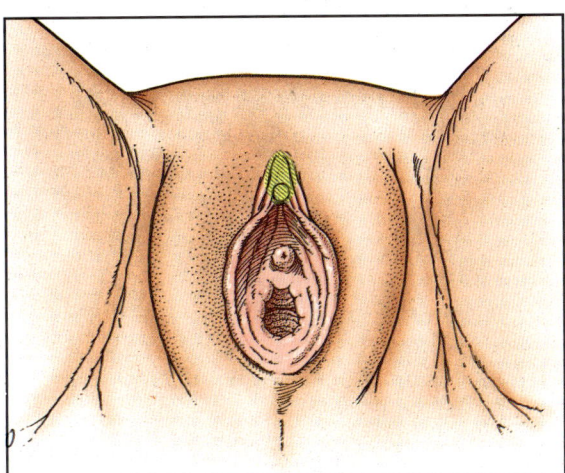

Type I: Clitoridectomy
(Yellow area indicates tissue to be removed.)

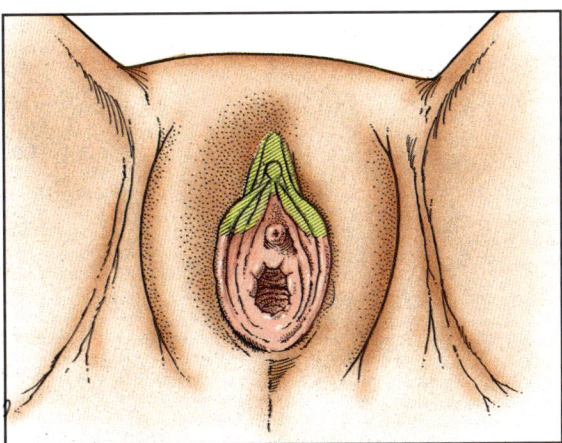

Type II: Excision
(Yellow area indicates tissue to be removed.)

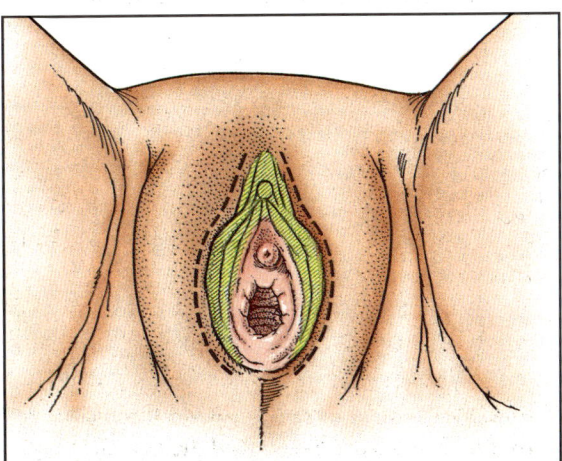

Type III: Infibulation (Yellow area to be removed; dotted line indicates labial incisions.)

cutting and suturing involved in this type of operation, physical, sexual, and psychological effects are numerous and long-lasting.

Although only an estimated 15 percent of all women who experience FGM have this type of operation, in certain countries, like Sudan, Somalia, and Djibouti, 80 to 90 percent of all FGM is infibulation. It is also practiced on a smaller scale in parts of Mali, Ethiopia, Eritrea, Gambia, and Egypt, and may be occurring in other communities where information is incomplete.

A new practice, known as intermediate circumcision, has come into use in recent years. Intermediate circumcision has evolved in countries where infibulation has been outlawed (such as Sudan) or where the impact of infibulation on women's health has been criticized. Nevertheless, this category of operations is quite similar to infibulation and the effects and complications are more or less the same; for this reason, these procedures are not considered a separate category in this text.

Terms such as Sunna[1] and Pharonic circumcision should not be used in scientific descriptions of FGM since they are colloquial terms in Arabic speaking countries only and do not indicate the extent of the cutting.

[1] "Sunna" refers to any practice regularly required of Muslims. The belief that female circumcision is required of Muslims is a serious misunderstanding in the interpretation of Islam, and has contributed to the spread of the practice. See the section on religion, page 31.

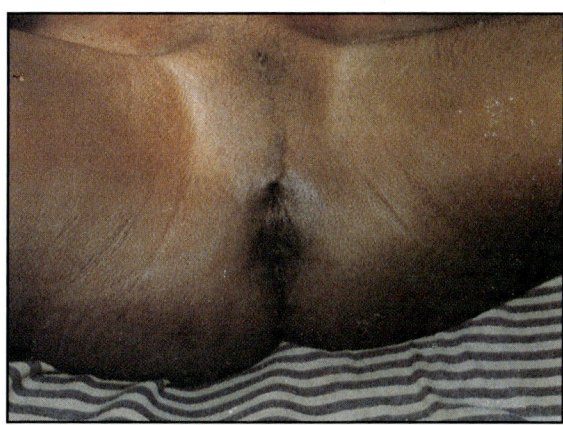

Seven-year-old Sudanese girl with infibulation.

"*I was circumcised in 1960, at the age of 11 years. I remember every detail of the operation and the worst part was when the wound became infected.... When I was 18 years old it was the turn of my younger sister; I was totally against her circumcision. My father wanted the Sunna type (clitoridectomy) but my mother insisted on the Pharonic (infibulation). Eventually my sister had the intermediate type, virtually the same as the Pharonic. The suffering of my sister made me hate circumcision even more than my own, earlier, experience.*"

—Dr. Asma El Dareer
The Sudanese physician who conducted the first national survey on FGM in Sudan, in the introduction to her book, *Woman, Why Do You Weep?*

What are the Complications and Effects of FGM?

It is important to remember that FGM is neither a disease nor a reproductive risk. It is a man-made problem that causes grave damage to women. All three types can have serious physical complications, although those resulting from infibulation generally occur more frequently and are more severe and long-lasting.

Complications of Type I & II

Bleeding

Amputation of the clitoris involves cutting across the clitoral artery, which supplies blood to the erectile, spongy tissue of the clitoris and its surroundings. This artery has a strong flow and high pressure. To stop bleeding, the artery must be packed tightly or tied with a suture, either of which may slip and lead to hemorrhage.

Hemorrhage may also occur after the first week as a result of sloughing of the clot over the artery, usually because of infection. Protracted bleeding commonly leads to anemia, which may, in turn, affect the growth of the child. If bleeding is very severe and uncontrolled, it can result in death.

Infection

Infection can be caused by unsterile cutting instruments or may occur within a few days as the area becomes soaked in urine and contaminated by feces.

Infection is very common. The degree of infection varies widely from a superficial film of pus, to an ulcerating wound, to a general toxic infection (septicemia) if the bacteria reaches the blood stream. If not treated promptly with strong antibiotics, septicemia often leads to death. Unsterilized equipment can lead to tetanus infection, which is also usually fatal.

There is no evidence that FGM is a major contributor to the spread of HIV infection, although it is reported that group circumcisions using the same unclean cutting instruments is still common. Repeat cutting and stitching and possibility of anal intercourse also increase the risk of AIDS.

Pain

The majority of operations are done without anesthetic. Even when local anesthesia is used, pain in the highly sensitive area of the clitoris returns within two to three hours of the operation. Although general anesthesia is rarely used, it poses a considerable risk for children in countries with few specialized anesthetists.

Local anesthesia in itself often becomes another form of torture. The clitoris is a highly vascular organ with a dense concentration of nerve endings. To anesthetize the area completely, multiple, painful insertions of the needle are required. The anesthetic used also produces a stinging sensation which can be painful. Many doctors or midwives who perform FGM prick the clitoris with just a few drops of anesthetic, more to satisfy the relatives—and to claim a higher fee—than to relieve the child's pain.

Urine Retention

Pain, swelling, and inflammation of the front of the vulva usually result in an inability to pass urine for hours or days. Urine retention increases pain and discomfort and can also cause urinary infection and back pain from pressure on the kidneys. These complications are usually temporary and are corrected when urine is passed normally again.

Stress and Shock

The pain, fear, and stress of screaming may cause the child to faint or enter a state of shock. Such traumatic shock can very occasionally cause death.

Damage to Urethra or Anus

This may be caused by an inexperienced circumciser or may occur accidentally if the girl moves suddenly while trying to get away. Such damage will cause problems for life.

Long-term Complications of Type I & II

Apart from the psychological effects, most wounds will heal with few long-term problems. However, for some women, the wound can become the site of an ongoing nightmare, which dominates their life for years. Cases have been reported where girls suffered repeated infections, soreness, and intermittent bleeding for many years. The stitch used to tie the clitoral artery may not be absorbed totally, becoming the focus for an abscess. A nerve ending may be scarred, leading to the formation of a neuroma, (a small benign tumor of the nerve), which causes intense pain. The tough scar over the clitoris may split open during childbirth.

Because extreme complications are not as common with clitoridectomy as they are with infibulation, they are usually ignored, and clitoridectomy is falsely perceived to be safe. In addition, because communities that practice FGM are exposed to a high risk of injuries and disease in general, fear of the health risk is not a strong deterrent, given the powerful social value associated with the practice.

Complications of Infibulation

All the complications of clitoridectomy are compounded by the extensive cutting and stitching associated with infibulation. Bleeding and the risk of hemorrhage are greater. The pain is more severe and less likely to be dulled with local anesthesia. Because the raw wound is larger, the risk of infection and stitch abscess is higher. Urine retention is also much more common, since the skin is stitched over the urethra, obstructing the normal flow. Urination remains painful for weeks.

Long-term Complications of Infibulation

Unlike clitoridectomy, the health problems of infibulation rarely disappear after the first healing. The following are some of the more commonly recorded long-term complications: repeated urinary infection; stones in the urethra and the bladder due to obstruction and repeated infections; excessive growth of scar tissue at the site, which may become disfiguring. In addition, dermoid cysts may form on the stitch line, caused by skin cells becoming embedded deep in the scar tissue. Cysts have been reported from the size of a pea to as large as a grapefruit, and must be removed by surgery.

If the false vaginal opening is very small, the menstrual flow is also obstructed, leading to frequent reproductive tract infections. Chronic pelvic

infection follows, with constant back and menstrual pain, irregularity, and vaginal discharge. Infertility is a common, devastating result, with profound repercussions in a society where a woman's reproductive capacity is central to her existence.

Pain during sexual intercourse is very common among infibulated women. It could be due to actual physical discomfort or because the woman finds intercourse psychologically traumatizing. Most likely, the two causes reinforce each other.

During childbirth, a tightly infibulated woman must be de-infibulated to allow the fetal head to crown. If a trained attendant is not available to cut the covering, the labor will be obstructed. Prolonged obstructed labor can cause life-threatening complications for both the mother and the child.

A Destiny of Cutting and Restitching

In addition to the physical complications described, the many cuttings and restitchings performed on infibulated women must be considered health risks in themselves. The recurring de- and re-infibulation begins with the wedding night, when the "hood" must often be cut open to allow intercourse.

A larger cut is necessary to allow childbirth. Additional cutting and stitching takes place with each birth—ten or 15 births are common in some countries where infibulation is practiced.

In effect, the delicate area where female genitals once existed is turned into tough scar tissue that bears more resemblance to cured hide than to human tissue. Women in these communities have no perception or experience of soft, tender female genitals on adult women.

As women age, their bodies become subject to a slew of new ailments, many of which are exacerbated by infibulation. Older women in their sixties or seventies—as well as their doctors and nurses—speak with distress about the ordeal of catheterization, for example, during the course of an illness.

Why is it important to differentiate between complications of different types of FGM?

Since the complications of Types I & II are less frequent and less severe than those for infibulation, well-meaning critics of FGM can fall into a trap when criticizing the operations. When health risk is cited as the major justification for eradication, the arguments ring false in communities where clitoridectomy or excision is the norm. This is particularly true when the messages are directed at the traditional or trained midwives, who have performed enough of the milder types to know that the most horrifying complications rarely occur. In addition, in areas where infibulation is common, government officials, the medical establishment, and local powerbrokers may promote clitoridectomy as a safer alternative that can be performed under hygienic conditions. This occurred in Sudan, but the policy was rejected by women activists as a regressive strategy.

The ultimate question is not which procedure should take place, but what kind of medical system or public health policy condones the cutting away of part of the human body for no beneficial reason? How can health professionals justify the risk that any kind of surgery entails, purely for the purpose of gender subjugation and perpetuation of social injustice?

Aziza Kamil, leader of the Cairo Family Planning Association's project on FGM, is one who has argued strenuously against recent attempts to promote milder forms of FGM, performed under medical supervision: ***"No action will entrench FGM more than legitimating it through the medical profession. If doctors and hospitals start to perform it, rather than condemn it, we will have no hope of ever eradicating the practice. All the respect and authority given to doctors will be transferred to the practice and we (activists) will lose our credibility."***

The Sexual and Psychological Effects of FGM

Removal of the clitoris takes away the primary specialized female sexual organ. The tip of the clitoris, like the tip of the penis, has a dense supply of nerve endings which are extremely sensitive to touch. The body of the clitoris is made of spongy erectile tissue with a covering layer of more sensory nerve endings and a rich blood supply from the clitoral artery. This erectile tissue spreads deep under the root of the clitoris, is found in the inner lips and on the floor of the vulva, and forms a ring around the entry to the vagina. Although this tissue does not have the same density of nerve endings as the tip of the clitoris, it is more sensitive than the surrounding skin. In comparison, the vagina has very few nerve endings, most of which are not sensitive to touch.

In humans, the ability to attain sexual pleasure—to achieve orgasm—is a complex process. It involves the presence of normal external genitals, appropriate hormonal stimulants, and individual psychology.

By altering the normal anatomy of the female sexual organs, FGM reduces the ease with which sexual fulfillment is achieved, or makes it extremely difficult. Unlike men's genitals, women's are clearly separated by function. The clitoris is a specialized sexual organ dedicated only to pleasure; it has no reproductive function. The vagina is an organ of reproduction with minimal sensory capacity for sexual response. In other words, FGM removes the woman's sexual organ, while her reproductive organs are left intact.

With clitoridectomy, some of the sensitive tissue at the base of the clitoris, along the inner lips and around the floor of the vulva are still intact and will give sensory sexual messages if properly stimulated. In addition, other sexually sensitive parts of the body, such as the breasts, nipples, lips, neck, and ears may become hypersensitized to compensate for lack of clitoral stimulation and thus enhance sexual arousal.

Infibulation may not leave the woman with any sexually sensitive genital tissue and, in compensation, substitute sensory areas have to be called upon to an even greater degree. While FGM does not affect the hormonal stimulants for sexual desire and arousal, it can obviously have a very negative effect on a woman's feeling about her right to sexual pleasure. Such psychological effects cannot be predicted in all cases and they may be overcome by some women.

The psychological aspect of human sexual arousal is an equally complex phenomenon which is still not fully understood by experts. It involves emotions, concepts of morality, past experience, acceptance of eroticism, fear of disease or pregnancy, dreams and fantasies. The combination of physical messages from sensory organs and the emotional images culminate in a psychophysiological state during which a person is able to experience orgasm.

If FGM is performed during infancy, it is unlikely that the girl will remember the event itself. Even if the trauma lingers deep in her subconscious, psychology cannot predict the extent to which this traumatic memory will be clearly linked to sexuality in her conscious mind.

Most circumcisions take place when a girl is older and already receiving multiple social messages about her position in society in general, and in regard to boys and men in particular. The link between the operation and the social feminization of women might be made through subtle, positive associations or through aggressive gender training and threats of negative consequences or even torture. The first model is more common in East Africa; the second is employed more often in West Africa, with its cults of "secret societies."

It would be difficult for any child above infancy not to associate circumcision with some diminution of sexual desire; the message and the act appear to be interrelated. With infibulation, in particular, the radical shaving off of all sensitive tissue plus the folding away of the vagina, can be seen as a metaphor for the denial of a woman's sexuality and the locking up of her reproductive capacity with a chastity belt made of her own flesh. The "protective hood" is only allowed to be cut open or dilated to permit the husband his lawful access to the vagina in return for his bride price. Later it is opened further when the woman is performing her sacred duty of childbirth.

Because women who have had either type of operation are likely to become sexually frustrated, they may no longer seek sexual contact with their partners. Ultimately, they become sexual objects and reproductive vehicles for men. This role conflicts with the social requirement that a woman be sexually desirable and pleasing to her husband, especially if sexual pleasing requires her to show that she, too, is enjoying the sexual experience.

It is difficult, of course, to verify the reports of circumcised women about their sexual experiences. Social proscriptions, the lost memory of what it is like to have a clitoris, plus the strong expectation that a woman must be satisfied with her husband's sexual approaches, prevents many women from speaking openly about their sexuality.

Because women's sexuality is made even more complex by cultural values and ambiguities, it is difficult to separate the purely anatomical and hormonal sexual functions from emotional and psychological influences. This means that a woman without a clitoris is still able to reach orgasm, although not with ease. In extensive interviews with highly educated and sexually informed women, this author was able to identify women with clitoridectomy or intermediate infibulation who do experience orgasm.

It is the combination of physical and psychological barriers that makes it difficult, but not impossible, for women who have experienced FGM to enjoy their sexuality. Those who are reportedly still able to achieve orgasm have the spirit to maintain the required psychosexual state, using maximum creativity and minimal resources. To continue enjoying partnership and sexual life under such

conditions is proof of women's vitality.

For those who have trouble imagining why a society would impose circumcision on its women, it might be useful to remember the impact of Freudian theories on Western women's sexuality. By labelling clitoral orgasms an "immature" fixation and glorifying vaginal orgasms achieved through intercourse, Freudian theory, in effect, imposed a psychological clitoridectomy on women. In the United States, a majority of women were unaware of the clitoris or its function as recently as the 1960s, and had difficulty experiencing orgasm.

Although nearly all societies subjugate women in some way, FGM is the most drastic measure taken by any society to control women's sexuality and reproduction. The starkness of the act and its severity is an important reminder of more subtle mechanisms that operate in other societies.

Psychological Complications

Most of the attention given to the health problems associated with FGM concentrate on the physical aspect, with little attention to the psychological problems. No studies have been conducted to measure the effect of the trauma on children. Indeed, compared to concern over problems such as malnutrition or diarrhea, there has been little discussion of the effect of this common practice on children, giving the impression that children of the developing countries have bodies but no psyches.

The psychological complications of FGM may be submerged deeply in the child's unconscious. However, many children do exhibit behavioral changes, and some problems may not become evident until the child reaches adulthood.

Dr. Taha Baashar, a senior psychologist from Sudan, has reported three cases of clinical psychological disease arising from FGM and its complications:

Case 1

A 7-year-old girl developed an "anxiety state" associated with lack of sleep and hallucinations caused by fear of the operation. The child's condition improved when she was reassured that she would not be circumcised.

Case 2

A 32-year-old married woman with three children was diagnosed as having "reactive depression" caused by delayed healing of the recircumcision scar following childbirth eight weeks previously.

Case 3

A 30-year-old nomadic woman was diagnosed as having "psychotic excitement". She was childless and twice-divorced. The woman had a dermoid cyst the size of a tennis ball over her infibulation scar, which covered the entrance to the vagina. She had never told her family about this problem.

Such cases can be only the tip of the iceberg. There are very few qualified psychologists and psychotherapists available to analyze these problems, nor are psychological disease and disturbances readily recognized in Africa. Psychological symptoms are often interpreted as the work of evil spirits. Traditional remedies and rituals are usually used to deal with these symptoms, without any understanding of the underlying problems. **Many women who may be traumatized by their circumcision experiences, worried about a physical complication, or fearful of sex have no acceptable means of expressing their feelings and suffer in silence. When the pressure reaches a certain level, their condition can progress to psychopathological levels.**

In the experience of this writer, who worked as a clinician in public hospitals in Sudan, thousands of women come to the Ob/Gyn outpatient clinics with vague chronic symptoms which they metaphorically interpret as originating from the pelvis. These women are perceived by doctors and the hospital authorities as a great nuisance and a drain on the system since they have no medically detectable pathology. Sitting for hours listening to them, it soon becomes clear that the vague symptoms of general fatigue, loss of sleep, backache, headache, pelvic congestion, uttered in a depressed, monotonal voice, are a muted cry for help for a much more deeply felt pain. With a little probing, the women talk about fear of sex, the threat of infertility after infection, and fears about the state of their genitals (they have no way of assessing whether they are normal). Yet, **these women's symptoms are labelled hysterical, their feelings dismissed as those of malingerers.**

"*Now, what is the justification of female circumcision? They think it diminishes sexual desire, so that means you will be faithful. They also say that female circumcision purifies women, that means that our sex genitalia is dirty.... To them, female circumcision is very necessary to support their view of women's sexuality.*"

—Assitan Diallo of Mali
Quoted in A. Gevins, "Tackling Tradition: African Women Speak Out Against Female Circumcision", in *Third World, Second Sex*, compiled by Miranda Davis

Where and to What Extent is FGM Practiced?

Estimates of the total number of women subjected to FGM in Africa range between 100 and 130 million. At the current rates of population increase, the estimated number of girls eligible for FGM is more than 2 million every year.[2]

Female genital mutilation was practiced by many cultures in the past, including the Phoenicians, Hittites, and the ancient Egyptians. **It was also used by modern physicians in England and the United States, as recently as the 1940s and 1950s, to "treat" hysteria, lesbianism, masturbation, and other so-called female deviances. At present it is reportedly practiced in at least 26 African countries, among a few groups in Asia and among some African immigrants in North and South America, Australia, and Europe.**

FGM is practiced by Muslims, Christians, some animists, and one Jewish sect, but it is not a requirement of any of these religions; the distribution of the practice does not follow the distribution of these religious groups on the African continent. A look at the map of countries where FGM is practiced shows a continuity of influence between neighboring cultures; the map does not follow the distribution of Islam or any other religion through Africa, helping to confirm that this is a practice of culture more than religion.

FGM was spread by dominant tribes and civilizations, often as a result of tribal, ethnic, and cultural allegiances. For example, FGM was not known in western Sudan among the Furs and the residents of the Nuba mountains up to the 1950s. After independence in 1956, local government, education, and health services were introduced in the region by professionals from the educated middle classes of the north where FGM was practiced. In the next twenty years, the cultural influences of the northern elites prevailed. A survey conducted in 1979 reported that in Fur and Nuba families, mothers were not circumcised, but most daughters were.

[2] Based on an analysis of trends from the Sudan DHS, and using four years as the initial age of risk, the number of girls at risk per year was calculated using the United Nations projections of female population in the affected African countries in 1995. If there is no decline from current prevalence, 2.5 million girls will be at risk per year. If there is a 10 percent decline, 2.2 million girls will be at risk per year. This crude estimate assumes that all concerned societies have the same age distribution for FGM and will experience the same socioeconomic, educational, and urbanization influences as Sudan, which was used as the standard for calculations because it is the only nation with detailed statistics.

Current Estimates of FGM

Documentation on the prevalence of different types of FGM began in the early twentieth century with reports by European travellers and missionaries. Since the 1950s, small studies have been undertaken by physicians and gynecologists in some countries, using either clinical case records or direct interview techniques. More recently, academicians and women's organizations have also conducted studies. While research on the subject has been neglected, limited findings suggest that the prevalence of FGM varies according to education, social class, and rural or urban dwelling and that it tends to be highest in poorer rural communities where educational opportunities are limited.

The first national survey ever to be undertaken was lead by Dr. Asma El Dareer in Sudan in 1979. The Sudan Fertility Survey of 1979 and the Sudanese Demographic and Health Survey in 1990 also included questions on FGM. Sudan remains the only country with reliable national prevalence data.

There is no comprehensive, country-by-country data collection on FGM. United Nations agencies do not collect statistics. The most extensive estimates have been reported by Ms. Fran Hosken, who has to date published four editions of the book titled "Hosken Report" (Fourth Edition 1993) and updates her estimates in a quarterly newsletter called WIN news. Ms. Hosken does not describe in any of her publications the methodology through which she reached her estimates. Still they are the most comprehensive figures available to date and the global estimates of FGM which appear in many publications are derived from these estimates. My own estimates are based on extensive review of published and unpublished studies most of which are not based on national samples. I have also relied on reporting through extensive communication with a network of activist organizations and health practitioners who are familiar with the situation in their countries. Where I have not found studies or reliable national experts I have quoted Ms Hosken's figures. These are marked with * in the table of prevalence.

The lack of definitive data on the prevalence of FGM is an indication of the neglect of the issue by the scientific community. While detailed questions on the complications of FGM or its effect on sexuality may not be appropriate for survey questionnaires, experience has shown that simple prevalence data would not be difficult to collect in national demographic surveys. We have assisted the Demographic and Health Surveys (DHS) in developing a module on prevalence of FGM in the mother and first born daughter and on attitude for and against FGM. It is hoped that DHS surveys in the concerned African countries within the next five years will generate better national statistics on FGM. The questionnaire module is available from RAINB♀ and from the DHS.

The map and table summarize available information about the geographic distribution and prevalence of Female Genital Mutilation in Africa. The map illustrates that FGM is practiced in a band that crosses Sub-Saharan Africa north of the equator. The table lists best available estimates on the prevalence of the practices and the population affected in each country.

Although clitoridectomy is the most common procedure by far, infibulation predominates in Somalia, Djibouti, and northern Sudan, as well as in southern Egypt and the costal areas of Ethiopia. FGM is not practiced in Southern Africa nor in the Arabic-speaking countries of North Africa, with the exception of Egypt. In addition, probably because of historical conflict, it is essentially nonexistent in southern Sudan.

Female Genital Mutilation in Africa

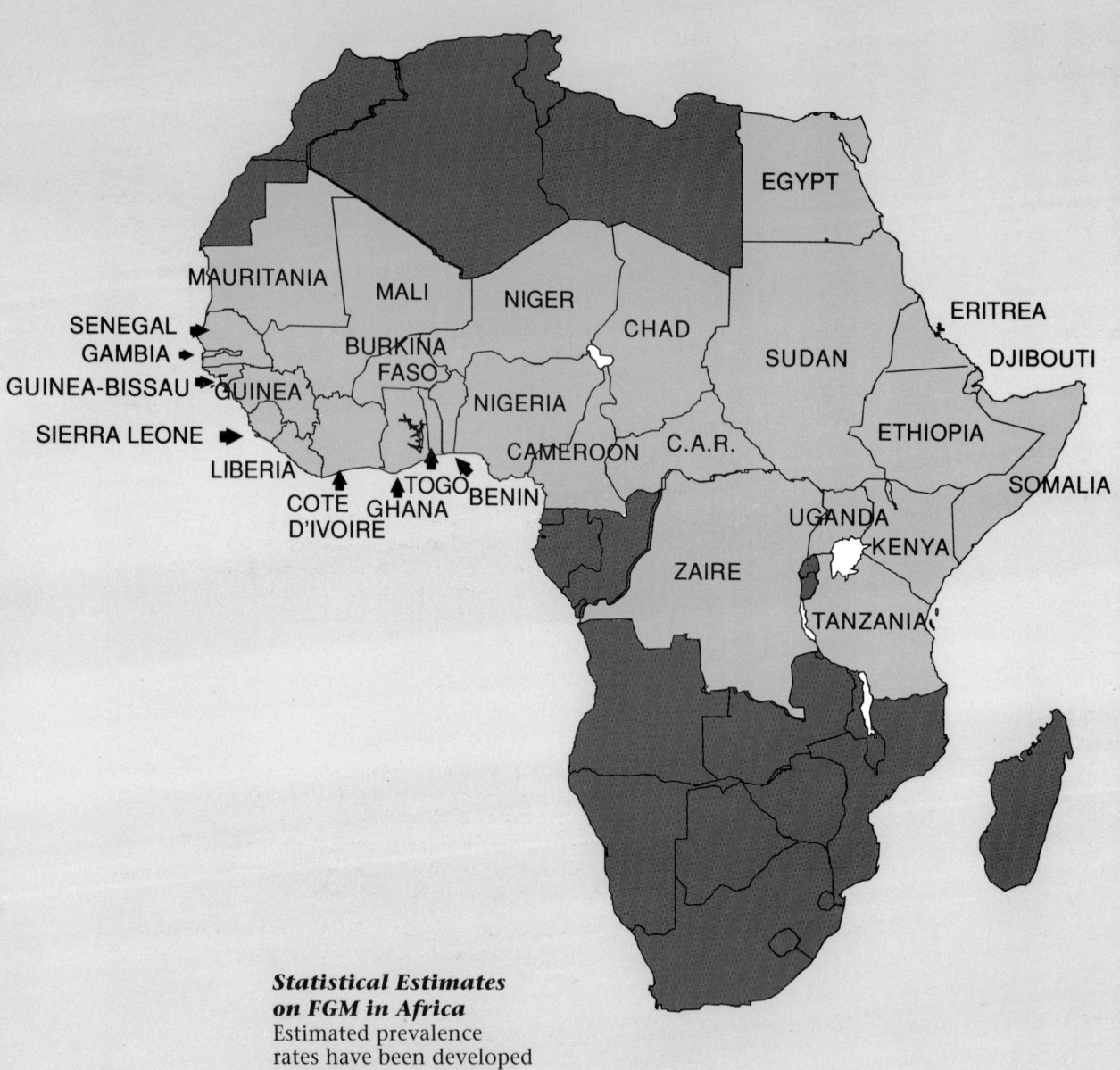

Statistical Estimates on FGM in Africa
Estimated prevalence rates have been developed from reviews of national surveys, small studies and country reports and from the Hosken Report, Fourth Edition, 1993.

Country	Prevalence	ACTUAL Number	Notes
Benin*	50%	1,200,000	
Burkina Faso	70%	3,290,000	From the national committee.
Cameroon	20%	1,310,000	From national group.
Central African Republic*	50%	750,000	
Chad	60%	1,530,000	Prevalence based upon 1990 and 1991 studies in three regions.
Côte d'Ivoire*	60%	3,750,000	
Djibouti	98%	196,000	Infibulation almost universally practiced.
Egypt	80%	21,440,000	Clitoridectomy & Excision practiced throughout the country by both Muslims and Christians. Infibulation in areas of south Egypt. Reported by Egyptian Task Force on FGM, 1995.
Ethiopia and Eritrea	90%	23,940,000	Common among Muslims and Christians and practiced by Ethiopian Jews (Falashas), most of whom now live in Israel. Excision is more common, except in areas bordering Sudan and Somalia, where infibulation seems to have spread.
Gambia	80%	360,000	Reported by BAFROW.
Ghana	30%	2,325,000	A 1987 pilot survey in one community showed that 97 percent of interviewed women above age 47 were circumcised, while 48 percent of those under 20 were not.
Guinea	50%	1,875,000	Correspondence.
Guinea Bissau*	50%	250,000	
Kenya	50%	6,300,000	Decreasing in urban areas, but remains strong in rural ones. 1992 studies in four regions by Mandalaeo Ya Wana Wake found that traditional practitioners usually operated on a group of girls without instrument cleanup increasing the risk of H.I.V.
Liberia*	60%	810,000	
Mali	80%	3,320,000	Report by CADEF.
Mauritania*	25%	262,500	
Niger*	20%	800,000	
Nigeria	60%	36,750,000	NNMW association national study. A 1994 community survey in the southwest by Ile Ife University reports a prevalence of 89%.
Senegal	20%	750,000	Predominantly in the north and southeast. Only a minority of Muslims, who constitute 95 percent of the population, practice FGM.
Sierra Leone	90%	1,935,000	All ethnic groups practice FGM except for Christian Krios in the western region and in the capital, Freetown.
Somalia	98%	3,773,000	FGM is universal; approximately 80 percent of the operations are infibulation.
Sudan	89%	9,220,400	From DHS survey, predominantly infibulation, throughout most of the northern, eastern and western regions. No FGM in 3 southern regions. A small decline in the 1980s with a clear shift from infibulation to clitoridectomy.
Tanzania	10%	1,345,000	Clitoridectomy reported only among the Christian Chagga groups near Mount Kilimanjaro.
Togo*	50%	950,000	
Uganda	5%	467,500	From National experts.
Zaire*	5%	945,000	
Total		**129,843,500**	*Anecdotal information only; no published studies.

FGM in ASIA

FGM is not practiced in the Middle East, nor in the countries of the Arabian Peninsula, with the exception of Yemen, where clitoridectomy is found among a few ethnic groups that had historically been traders with countries in East Africa across the Red Sea.

India & Pakistan

Clitoridectomy is practiced by a small ethno-religious minority with a total population of a half million. This group, the Daudi Bohra of the Ismaili Shiaa sect, adopted Islam from Egypt and live in Western India. Other Muslim groups in India do not practice FGM nor is it practiced in the Muslim state of Pakistan except to the extent that some Bohra Muslims may move in and out from India.

Indonesia

Genital cutting operations existed in the past, but are no longer performed. A series of ritual clitoral ceremonies persist, which include cleaning and applying substances around the clitoris, symbolic (although not actual) cutting, or light puncture of the clitoris. Apparently, no permanent physical damage results from these rituals. According to the classification used in this publication, these practices, as currently described, are not considered genital mutilation.

Malaysia

Several writers mention genital practices among some Muslims in Malaysia, but no report from that country was ever documented or whether, if they exist, these rituals are of the cutting or non-cutting types.

Immigrant Populations

West African immigrants from various ethnic groups, and all social and educational levels, have been settling in the industrialized nations in great numbers since the time of colonialism.

Recently, the repeated civil wars and famines in the Horn of Africa have driven tens of thousands of Somali, Ethiopian, Eritrean, and Sudanese refugees to seek asylum in Europe, Canada and the United States. Although accurate numbers are hard to come by, in the U.S., for example, rough estimates indicate that approximately 15,000 immigrants from the Horn of Africa entered the country from 1990 to 1993. FGM is a common practice among the immigrant populations in these countries. (*See Map on page 34 for global distribution of FGM.*)

Between 1984 and 1990, the Israeli government undertook a major resettlement program for the entire Jewish population of Ethiopia. These Ethiopian Jews, or Falashas, were known to perform FGM, but there are no reports on current practices in Israel, nor has the government made any policy statements concerning FGM.

There have been reports from Brazil that immigrant women are undergoing FGM in Sao Paulo, but these reports have not yet been verified.

The United Nations High Commission for Refugees (UNHCR) has not produced any statements on FGM. There is also no evidence that UNHCR conducts any informational or cultural orientation programs to prepare refugees for the different attitudes and laws regarding FGM in the countries where they will be relocated.

The issue of FGM poses several challenging questions to the host country. Among them are:
a) How will gynecological, obstetric, and psychological health services handle genitally mutilated women?
b) Should the social and health services and law-enforcing agencies act to protect girl children from being circumcised?

The work of Efua Dorkenoo, the director of The Foundation for Women's Health, Research, and Development (FORWARD) and her colleagues in England provides a successful model for consideration by other countries. Their multidirectional approach combines community action, legal reform, and professional training for health and social service workers. The government in the United Kingdom has supported organizations of immigrant women to lead the work within their own communities, including developing training material and designing policy guidelines. Similar programs are now being adopted in France, where the Groupe Femme pour l'Abolition des Mutilations Sexuelles, organized by African women, reported that in 1992 there were 27,000 immigrant women and girls in France who had already undergone FGM or were at risk of it.

The Australian government recently began a humanitarian program to resettle Somali refugees. Officials are planning programs to educate new settlers against FGM and considering introducing anti-FGM legislation.

"You are the young wife, my daughter. You are beautiful my daughter. I will be gentle with you. Don't be afraid. It is painful no doubt, but the pain disappears like hunger. You know what?" and she turned to Efuru's mother-in-law. "You know Nwakaego's daughter?"

"Yes, I know her."

"She did not have her bath [circumcision] before she had that baby who died after that dreadful flood."

"God forbid. Why?"

"Fear. She was afraid. Foolish girl. She had a foolish mother, their folly cost them a son."

—From "Efuru", a novel by Flora Nwapa
Nigeria's first-published woman novelist, 1966

Who Performs FGM?

FGM is performed by different practitioners in different areas. Traditionally, the role of circumciser is an inherited one, performed by female laypeople. (Some men perform FGM, but this is uncommon.)

In many rural communities, the traditional birth attendant (TBA) is the circumciser. In more recent years, medically trained midwives and nurses have taken over from the traditional practitioners and have played an important role in legitimizing the practice. They use their prestige and knowledge of antisepsis, local anesthesia, and sterile suturing to win over the more affluent clientele from the traditional birth attendants. Trained midwives commonly use medical supplies provided to them by ministries of health or UNICEF programs and meant to improve childbirth care.

Doctors are also increasingly providing circumcision services, although most medical associations condemn the practice. Small surgical procedures like clitoridectomy bring in revenue with little effort or expectation of long-term followup. As African economies deteriorate, the extra income that circumcision can bring becomes even more important. Doctors are taking over this lucrative market from midwives by arguing that they can reduce the health risks.

The vested interests of many circumcisers play a role in the continuation and spread of FGM. For example, in Sudan and Gambia, circumcisers are usually traditional practitioners or trained health personnel who come from poor families and/or ethnic groups with low social status. The income from FGM is many times what they could earn as a mere nurse or midwife. Since circumcisers perform such a highly valued service, their status also improves. Persuading these practitioners to abandon FGM on the basis of humanitarian appeals or financial compensation that is only a fraction of their income will not succeed. They will have to be compensated for the loss of income and prestige on a scale equivalent to that loss.

In Sierra Leone, circumcisers are highly respected women leaders who control the traditional secret societies. To their followers, they are priestesses. Although these women have never been treated as social inferiors, they hold too much power and wealth to easily agree to give up their position.

"With regard to abolishing female circumcision, it is important that there be a final religious announcement clearly stating that it is a form of mutilation and therefore forbidden. It is not sufficient for religion to shun female circumcision. Religion should be used as a tool for condemning and preventing its occurrence. The participation of women in the reinterpretation [of religion] will be crucial."

—Asma M. A'Haleem
"Claiming Our Bodies and Out Rights: Exploring
Female Circumcision as an Act of Violence," in
Freedom from Violence, edited by Margaret Schuler

Is FGM a Religious Practice?

FGM is a practice of culture, not religion. However, it is often strongly associated with Islam, because some African Muslim communities cite religion as the reason for performing it, and because Westerners have mistakenly related FGM to Islam.

Islam and FGM

Female Genital Mutilation is primarily found in Africa and those countries that have been influenced by African culture. There is no question that FGM preceded Islam in Africa. When Islam entered Africa, it is most likely that newly converted leaders, seeking to continue the practice of FGM, linked it with Islam. Over time, a belief was created in the minds of Muslims in these countries that FGM was required by Islam.

There is no major Islamic citation that makes female genital mutilation a religious requirement. Neither the Quran, the primary source for Islamic law, nor the "hadith," which are collections of the sayings of the Prophet Mohammed recorded from oral histories after his death, include a direct call for FGM. Mohammed's directive that is most often cited as a reason for circumcision is from a question during a speech; it is not one of the Prophet's lessons. And even here, when Mohammed was asked what he thought of female circumcision, his answer was, in essence, an attempt to deter the practice: He is said to have told his listeners to circumcise, but not to destroy (or mutilate), for not destroying (the clitoris) would be better for the man and would make the woman's face glow. Many people believe this describes a male-type circumcision where the prepuce is removed, with the object of making the clitoris even more sensitive to touch.

If this interpretation and the authenticity of the speech are accepted, this attitude toward women's sexuality on the part of Islam would not be surprising. In contrast to other major religions, Islam strongly acknowledges women's sexuality and emphasizes their right to sexual satisfaction as long as it is confined to marriage.

Islam also has different levels of religious requirements. The highest involves mandatory practices—the person who does not follow them is not considered a

Muslim. At the second level are practices that are strongly recommended; a Muslim must strive to adhere to them or be subject to punishment. On the third level are "makrama," practices that are not essential; if a Muslim adopts them, he or she receives extra points of merit, but if they are neglected, a follower of Islam will not be punished. Thus, even for those who accept the direction implied in Mohammed's speech, circumcision for women in Islam is classified as a "makrama."

Most of those who practice FGM are not religious scholars and do not know these basic facts. To combat FGM among Muslim people, authoritative religious interpretations along the lines described above must be prepared in a manner accessible to ordinary people.

Not only is there no specific call for FGM in the Quran, but the procedure is not practiced in predominantly Islamic countries such as Saudi Arabia, Iraq, the Gulf States, Kuwait, Algeria, and Pakistan. In fact, people from Muslim countries that do not practice FGM react with surprise when they hear about it and find it difficult to believe that genital mutilation is linked to Islam as they know it.

The transmission route of FGM helps to clarify it as a nonreligious practice. When Islam entered Asian countries from Arabia or Iran, it did not carry FGM with it, but when it was imported to Asia through Nile Valley cultures, FGM was a part of it. This was the case with the Daudi Bohra of India, whose religious beliefs are derived from an Egyptian-based sect of Islam.

Christianity and FGM

When Christian missionaries came to Africa along with the colonizers, they encountered FGM. The two major denominations in Africa were the Roman Catholic Church and Protestant Evangelists.

The Bible does not mention FGM, and formally at least, the Roman Catholic Church ignored it. At times, however, priests implicitly condoned the practice as a way to maintain women's sexual purity, an issue of great importance to the Church.

The Protestant church took a more active position that FGM was harmful. A few Christian leaders raised the issue in the British Parliament. In Sudan, for example, frequent reports to the colonial administration lead to the passing of a law against infibulation in 1946.

The early position of the two churches toward FGM affects Christian Africans today. Many followers of the Protestant church tend not to utilize the practice, and speak out against it more readily than Catholics.

Eventually, Africans created independent churches that were not formally allied with any Western sect. These churches actively promoted traditional customs, and, partly as a response to the missionaries' patronizing attacks on African culture, supported genital mutilation as an important link to past glories.

Another Christian denomination has existed on the African continent for centuries. Different sects of this Orthodox, or Coptic, church exist primarily in Egypt, Sudan and Ethiopia. Coptic leadership has maintained total silence regarding FGM, despite the fact that the majority of Copts live in areas where FGM is very common, and studies from Egypt and northern Sudan do, in fact, confirm that Coptic Christians perform both clitoridectomy and infibulation. In the Ethiopian Orthodox Church, some priests consider a woman unclean if she is not circumcised, and may refuse to let her enter their church.

Judaism and FGM

As is the case with the Quran and the Bible, the Torah has no specific mention of female circumcision. To date the only Jews known to practice FGM are the Ethiopian Falashas, who now live in Israel.

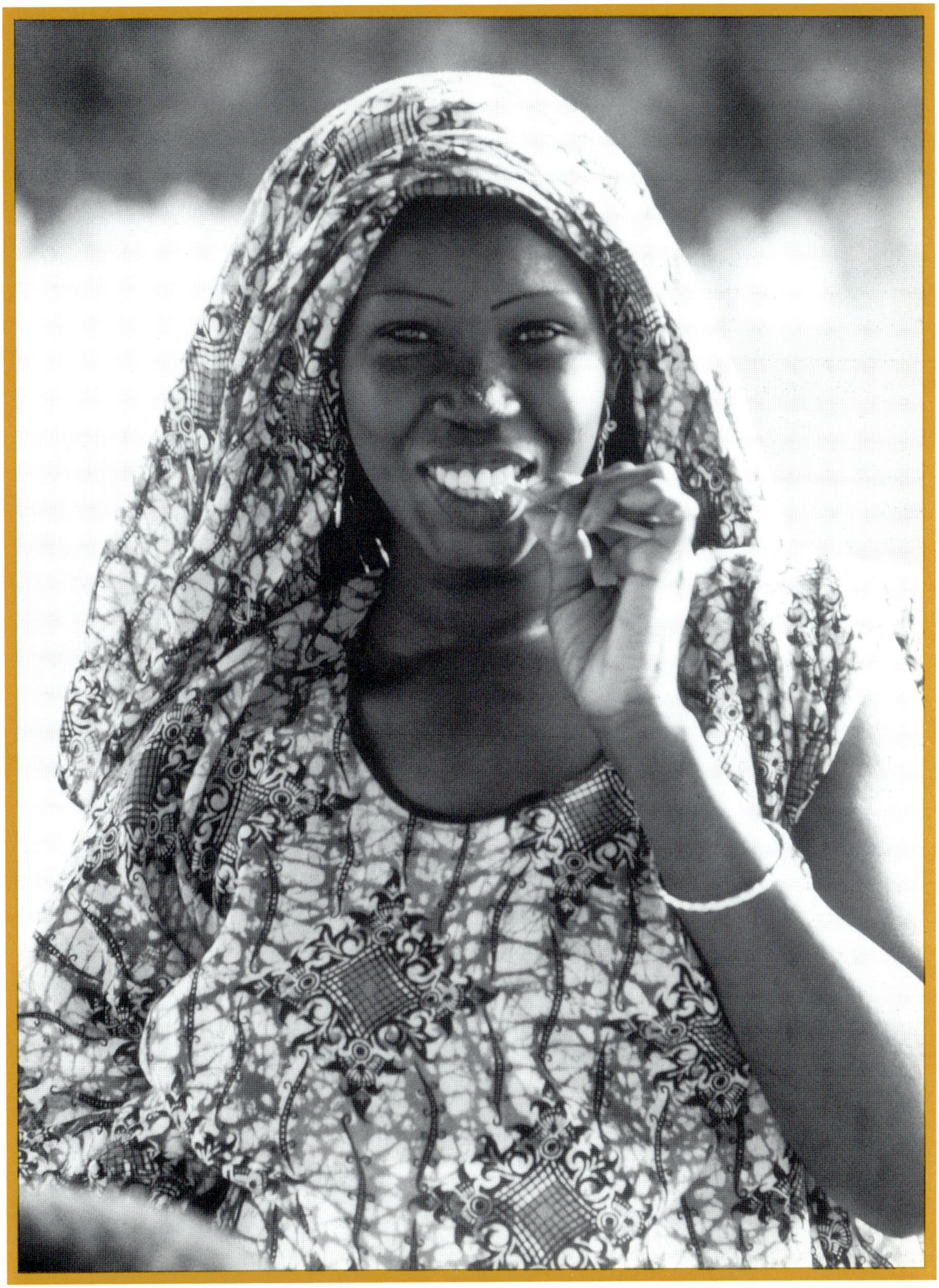

Global Distribution of FGM

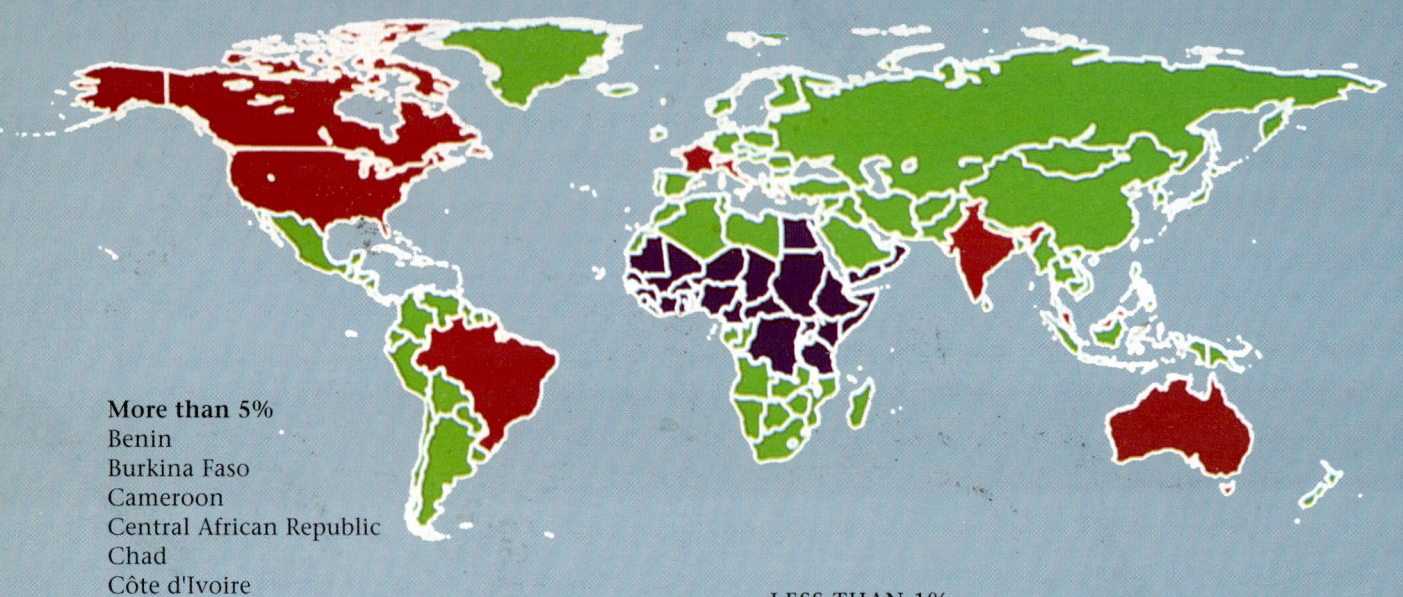

More than 5%
Benin
Burkina Faso
Cameroon
Central African Republic
Chad
Côte d'Ivoire
Djibouti
Egypt
Eritrea
Ethiopia
Gambia
Ghana
Guinea
Guinea-Bissau
Kenya
Liberia
Mali
Mauritania
Niger
Nigeria
Oman
Senegal
Sierra Leone
Somalia
Sudan
Tanzania
Togo
Uganda
Yemen
Zaire

LESS THAN 1%
Australia
Brazil
Canada
France
India
Israel
Italy
Netherlands
Sweden
United Kingdom
United States

Blue: *Practicing Population more than 5%*

Red: *Practicing Population less than 1%*

Green: *Nonpracticing countries*

The Cultural Significance of FGM

FGM will not be eradicated unless those who are fighting for change understand the deeply felt beliefs of the people who practice it. An important argument for retaining FGM is that it is part of adolescent initiation rites, which produce responsible adults for the community. African opponents of FGM believe that these rites have been so altered in the modern world that in many areas they have been reduced merely to the symbolic act of FGM. Africans now face the struggle to save the positive aspects of initiation rites, while eliminating damaging practices that subjugate women.

It is unfortunate that FGM is also used to stir up the historical rivalry between the Euro/American, Christian culture and the Afro/Arab, Muslim civilization. Cultural slander and stereotyping only makes real change more difficult to achieve. Some Western media highlight the link between FGM and Islam and call the practice "primitive and barbaric." Some reactionary elements in the African and Arab media retaliate by highlighting the decadence and disintegration of Western society, pointing especially to liberated women who are considered to be sexually promiscuous. Moreover, when African and Arab women speak out against FGM, they are accused by conservatives of aligning with the West to undermine the traditional (and religious) values of their societies. The battle is in fact about power and dominance, and finding a way to justify the abuse of others, particularly women.

In the few studies conducted on the subject, when researchers asked men and women why they performed genital mutilation, the answers were surprisingly clear about the patriarchal underpinnings of the practice and the ways in which women come to accept their secondary status. A constantly reiterated theme was the inferiority of women—a fact women and men both seem to accept. These messages are not so different from some that appear in the popular media in western countries. **The thinking of an African woman who believes "FGM is the fashionable thing to do to become a real woman" is not so different from that of an American woman who has breast implants to appear more feminine.**

Following are some of the reasons given for FGM. They are paraphrased and

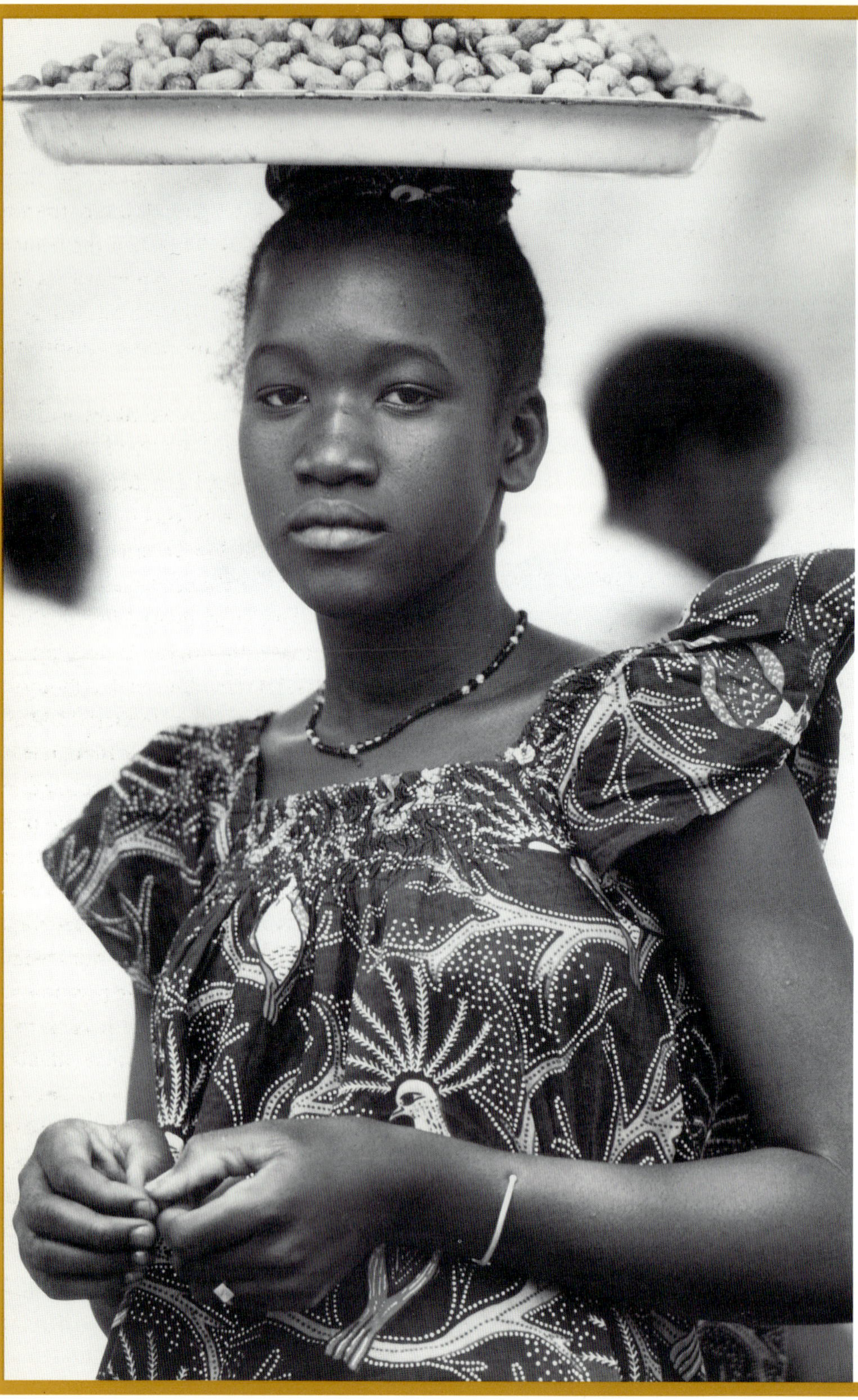

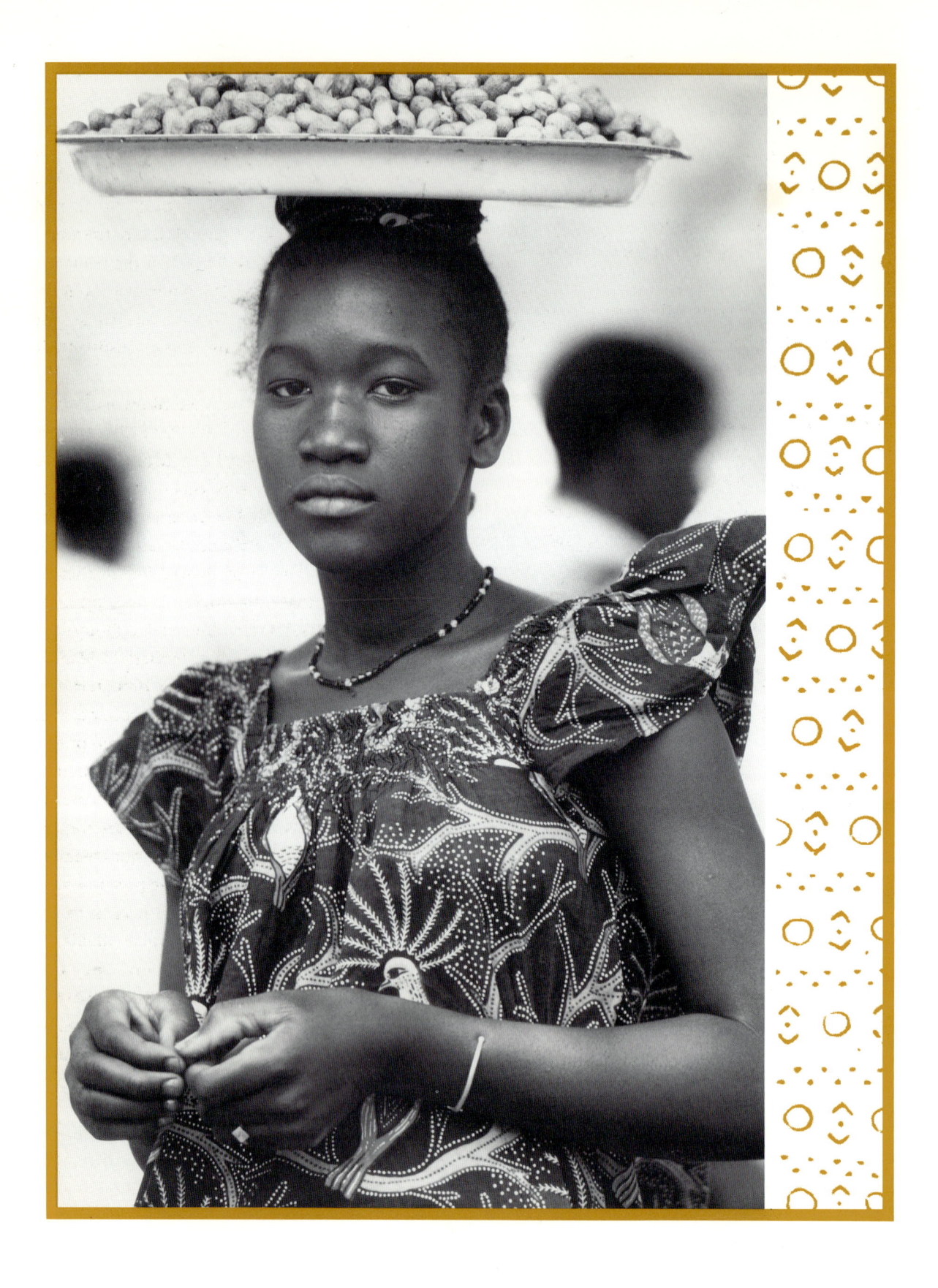

broken down into categories to enable the reader to see the commonalities among the various themes.

Beauty/Cleanliness
- Female genitals are unhygienic and need to be cleaned.
- Female genitals are ugly and will grow to become unwieldy if they are not cut back.
- FGM is the fashionable thing to do to become a real woman.

Male Protection/Approval
- FGM is an initiation into womanhood and into the tribe.
- The noncircumcised cannot be married.
- FGM enhances the husband's sexual pleasure.
- FGM makes vaginal intercourse more desirable than clitoral stimulation.

Health
- FGM improves fertility and prevents maternal and infant mortality.

Religion
- God sanctifies FGM.

Morality
- FGM safeguards virginity.
- FGM cures "sexual deviance," i.e., frigidity, lesbianism, and excessive sexual arousal.

None of the underlying messages and language used to justify FGM is unique to Africa. These messages reflect a universal language used to perpetuate women's second-class status and are reminiscent of reasons given for slavery, colonialism, and racism.

To understand why many women defend a practice that risks their health and damages their sexuality, we have to understand that even the most highly educated individuals become defensive when they feel their culture and personal identity are being attacked. Tribal and clan behavior can be observed among Sudanese women as well as executive secretaries in the United States, among adolescents in New York City or in Khartoum. The fear of losing the psychological, moral, and material benefits of "belonging" is one of the greatest motivators of conformity. When the demands of conformity conflict with rationality or individual need, denial intervenes as a mechanism for survival. In this way, many women justify their own oppression.

To defend themselves from feelings of inferiority, many African women deny that FGM damages their bodies or their sexuality. Africans who love and cherish the positive aspects of their cultures and have been wounded by colonialism fear that actions against FGM will be used as another excuse to invade and humiliate them. And finally, there is the simple fact that self-criticism is fine, but criticism by others is less tolerable even if both sides are in agreement. To conquer these barriers, FGM must be recognized as one form, extreme though it may be, among many forms of social injustice to women. In the Ethiopian Orthodox Church, some priests consider a woman unclean if she is not circumcised, and may refuse to let her enter their church.

Comparing FGM and cosmetic plastic surgery or even the wearing of high heels is not meant to trivialize the enormous physical and psychological damage FGM causes, but to relate it back to the ways all women suffer from false ideals of "femininity". **However, there is one very important difference between FGM and the ways in which women alter their bodies in other cultures: FGM is mainly performed on children, with or without their consent.**

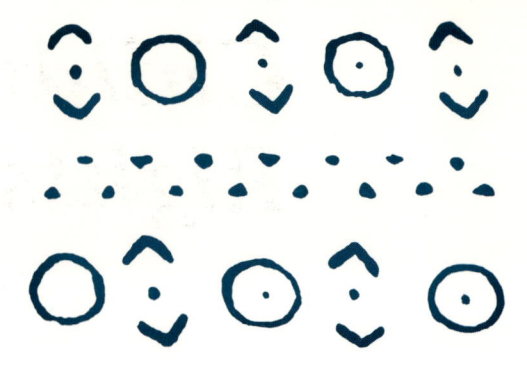

"The health hazards and psychological risks to children (as well as to women) of female circumcision are a sociocultural, health, and human rights problem. It is a human rights problem because 99 percent of the victims were forced into having the operation without prior knowledge of what it involves."

—Saffiatou K. Singhateh
*Former Executive Secretary,
Gambia Women's Bureau*

FGM and Children's Rights

Although FGM has been discussed at both international and national levels as a women's health and human rights issue, little thought has been given to it as an abuse of children. In October 1994, as a response to the call to Global Action, UNICEF issued an executive directive declaring that FGM is a health hazard to children and a violation of their human rights.

No research has been done on the meaning of the event to children or the effect it has on them, and for obvious reasons, reports by women who say circumcision makes a girl happier and better adjusted are suspect. Although a girl's response to the ritual cutting of her genitals may vary, there is little doubt that the loss of sexual organs affects physical health, psychological well-being, and future sexuality. In 1979, at the World Health Organization's Seminar on Traditional Practices Affecting the Health of Women and Children, Dr. A. H. Taba, former Regional Director of the WHO Eastern Mediterranean Region, made the following statement concerning the health risks of FGM:

> *"It is self-evident that any form of surgical interference in the highly sensitive genital organs constitutes a serious threat to the child, and that the painful operation is a source of major physical as well as psychological trauma. The extent and nature of the immediate and long-term mental disturbances will depend on the child's inner defences, the prevailing psychosocial environment, and a host of other factors. The family no doubt does its best to mitigate the painful effects of the operation; nonetheless, the child necessarily undergoes an overwhelming experience.*
>
> *Even before the operation, the threat of 'cutting' and [the] fear-provoking situation may disturb the mental state of the child to the degree [that] it causes worry, anxiety, sleeplessness, nightmares or panic. As anticipatory precautions against these anxieties, the family commonly uses various forms of traditional magico-religious practices such as fumigation, or the wearing of amulets."*

There is abundant evidence from clinics and hospital wards of the suffering experienced by girls from complications of infibulation. The physical scars get bigger, thicker, more painful or more callous with intercourse and childbirth. Do these scars symbolize a parallel set of invisible psychological scars?

Some writers have suggested that girls and women in certain societies accept suffering as part of their sense of womanhood, and that FGM gives them pride and membership in the community of women without any negative psychological effects. The little research that exists in this area suggests that despite the systematic subjugation and indoctrination of women to accept their own suffering, FGM still has a profound psychological impact on women and girls. A great deal of anecdotal evidence in support of this premise can be found in the stories of girls and women who have undergone FGM.

The conflict of feelings created in the child prior to her operation must be considerable. On the one hand, there is the desire to please parents, grandparents and relatives by doing something that is highly valued and approved of. Before the event, there is the desire to be "normal"—that is, to be like other members of society, particularly the peer group. This feeling is juxtaposed to the girl's expectation of pain, the stories of suffering, and the sheer terror of hearing the screaming of other children being circumcised. Finally, there is the experience itself: being held down by force while part of the body is cut off.

> "After the circumcision and a month of confinement Oumie was returned home. Yassin, her mother noticed that Oumi behaved very strangely; she was easily irritated, her appetite had gone, and she often kept herself in isolation. She also noticed that she was not comfortable when she sat for lunch. She asked what was wrong and the answer was 'Nothing'. Oumi was too embarrassed to mention her genitals in front of the other children. When Oumi's gloominess and discomfort got worse, and her visits to the toilet became frequent, her mother persuaded her to let her examine her genitals. There was inflammation and soreness at the site of the circumcision. It was three months after the operation. For a while Yassin tried the treatment of the Ngasimba (the traditional circumciser), but the wound got septic. She took her to the hospital where they dressed the wound and gave her antibiotics. The wound healed eventually, but the infection keeps recurring. Oumi has to visit the hospital two to three times a year. Yassin is accused by the Ngasimba of sabotaging the (secret) society and exposing its secrets".
>
> —From "The Story of Oumi, a 12-year-old Girl from Gambia," in "Circumcision in Gambia," by Saffiatou K. Singhateh, collected in *Female Circumcision: Strategies to Bring About Change*, The Somali Women's Democratic Organization

The fact remains that, in spite of the festivities, gifts, and peer rivalry surrounding the ceremony of FGM, most children experience it as a painful event. Some adults remember the operation as if it happened yesterday, while others erase it from their memories. Some become angry when confronting memories of the event, and others deny its effects altogether. All of these are classic responses to severe trauma.

Beyond the obvious effects on sexuality, researchers must explore the indirect impact of FGM in shaping girls' self-images. It could be argued that the long-term impact of annihilating an essential part of a girl's anatomy affects her ability to assume leadership roles in the future. Since development initiatives, for example, require the mobilization and empowerment of women, FGM could also be considered a hindrance to economic growth.

Further complicating the issue is the fact that children also suffer if they are prevented from participating in peer groups.

> "When girls of my age were looking after the lambs, they would talk among themselves about their circumcision experiences and look at each other's genitals to see who had the smallest opening. If there was a girl in the group who was still uninfibulated, she would always feel ashamed since she had nothing to show the others. Every time the other girls showed their infibulated genitals, I would feel ashamed I was not yet circumcised. Whenever I touched the hair of infibulated girls, they would tell me not to touch them since I was 'unclean' because I had not yet been circumcised and shaved. After the infibulation the girls hair is shaved and washed in a special way as a rite of purification, but my hair was dirty.
>
> One day I could not stand it anymore. I took a razor blade and went to an isolated place. I tied my clitoris with a thread, and while pulling at the thread with one hand I tried to cut part of my clitoris. When I felt the pain and saw the blood coming from the cut I stopped and went directly to my paternal aunt (my own mother was dead) and told her what I had done. I had heard my grandmother tell how she had tried to infibulate herself in order to hasten the process, and now I had tried to repeat what my grandmother had done.
>
> After some weeks, I was infibulated together with seven other girls. I was seven years old, but some of the other girls were older. After a few days the wound healed and the thorns were removed. When I was able to resume my normal work, I felt proud, and whenever some girls asked me if I was infibulated, I did not have to hide my genitals."

—Anab's story from "Social and Cultural Implications of Infibulation in Somalia," by Amina Warsame, *Female Circumcision: Strategies to Bring About Change*, The Somali Women's Democratic Organization

The social penalties and individual pain that can result from nonconformity are serious considerations for those wishing to pioneer change for their children. Parents must be equipped with the means to deal with their children's fear of being different. One way to deal with the issue of peer approval is the use of role models—finding authority figures who disapprove of FGM and whom children and young people would be happy to emulate.

"*Women are victims of outdated customs, attitudes and male prejudice. This results in negative attitudes of women about themselves. There are many forms of sexual oppression, but this particular one is based on the manipulation of women's sexuality in order to assure male domination and exploitation. The origins of such practices may be found in the family, society, and religion.*"

—Raqiya Haji Dualeh Abdalla
*Somali Women's Democratic Organization,
World Health Organization seminar, Khartoum, 1979*

A Global Call to Action

The eradication of FGM requires global action. There are many people the world over who would like to see the genital mutilation of women stopped. Their concerns and efforts must be linked so that resources and knowledge can be shared, and so women are not forced to fight isolated battles against their own social and economic powerlessness—a powerlessness that allows FGM to continue. The Research, Action & Information Network for Bodily Integrity of Women (RAINB♀) has started the Global Action Against Female Genital Mutilation as a joint effort with Columbia University, School of Public Health.

Reports and research tell us much about what FGM is, how, why, and by whom it is performed. We have rough estimates of how many women and girls are subjected to it, and where they live. But we must learn more. **We must get exact information on prevalence, physical and psychological effects, and religious requirements. Most of all, this information must be accessible to a broad range of people and disseminated on a wide scale.**

FGM must be separated from the notion that it has a religious basis, while efforts to preserve cultural integrity must be honored. The task will be all the more difficult because individuals and communities are being asked to take action against a long-standing practice that is part of a heritage of which they are proud.

The Global Action Against FGM (GAAFGM) project is undertaking these tasks and many more.

We aim to combine local knowledge and sensibility with international technical and financial resources to create a multitude of programs. FGM would be linked to programs on women's economic development, human rights, health, family planning, child health and education. The work of indigenous activists, scholars, and sympathetic religious leaders, among others, could serve as an important source of valuable information. The common link among these efforts would be the extensive use of indigenous mass information, popular art and culture to create a multidirectional campaign.

Eradication efforts must be empathic, not alienating. They must recognize all forms of cultural manipulation and mutilation of women's bodies, whether physical or psychological. **Some of the defensiveness and anger expressed by Africans is caused by the manner in which opposition to FGM has been expressed.** The people of the countries where FGM is practiced resent references to "barbaric practices imposed on women by male-dominated primitive societies," especially when they look at the Western world and see women undergoing their own feminization rites. Both the message and the facts about FGM will be lost if advocates use the language of superiority—the language of the colonizer or slave holder.

Official Anti-FGM Action in Affected Countries

Country	CRC / CEDAW	African Charter	Laws / Regulations	Official Statements and Policy	Professional Regulations or Involvement
Australia	✓ | ✓		✚		
Belgium	✓ | ✓		▲		
Benin	✓ | ✓	✓		✓	
Burkino Faso	✓ | ✓	✓		✓	
Cameroon	✓ | s	s		✓	
Canada	✓ | ✓		✚		■
Ctrl African Republic	✓ | ✓	✓		✓	
Chad	✓	✓		✓	
Côte d'Ivoire	✓ | s		✚		
Djibouti	✓			✓	
Egypt	✓ | ✓	✓	✓	✓	
Ethiopia/Eritrea	✓ | ✓			✓	
France	✓ | ✓		✗		
Gambia	✓	✓		✓	
Ghana	✓ | ✓	✓	✓		✓
Guinea	✓ | ✓	✓	✚	✓	
Guinea Bissau	✓ | ✓	✓			
Italy	✓ | ✓		✚	✓	✚
Kenya	✓ | ✓			✓	
Liberia	s | ✓	✓		✓	
Mali	✓ | ✓	✓		✓	
Netherlands	s | ✓		✚	✓	●
Niger	✓ | ✓	✓		✓	
Nigeria	✓ | ✓	✓		✓	●
Norway	✓ | ✓			✓	
Senegal	✓ | ✓	✓		✓	
Sierra Leone	✓	✓		✓	
Somalia					
Sudan	✓	✓	✓	✓	●
Sweden	✓ | ✓			✓	
Togo	✓ | ✓	✓		✓	●
United Kingdom	✓ | ✓		✓	✓	■
United States	✓ | ✓		▲	✓	●
Yemen	✓ | ✓	✓			

CRC = Convention on the Rights of the Child (1990) (ratified March 1993).
CEDAW = Convention to Eliminate All Forms of Discrimination Against Women (1981) (ratified March 1993).
African Charter = African Charter of Human and People's Rights (1981) (ratified January 1990).
It should also be noted that the African Charter on the Rights and Welfare of the Child was adopted by the Organization of African Unity (OAU) in 1990. Individual states should be urged to ratify.

s = Signed but not ratified.
NATIONAL LAWS/REGULATIONS/CASE LAW:
✓ = legislation or ministerial regulations against FGM per se
✗ = FGM falls under existing legislation or application of case law
✚ = government official has stated FGM would fall under existing legislation, application of case law, or regulation
▲ = FGM could be prosecuted under existing legislation concerning child abuse, assault or battery causing bodily harm
PROFESSIONAL REGULATIONS AND INVOLVEMENT:
■ = professional regulations against FGM
● = involvement in or movement toward shaping professional standards against performing FGM operations

Legal Remedies

International action

International standards applicable to the issue of female genital mutilation are already in place. In addition to various pertinent international and regional human rights conventions and declarations, most affected countries have ratified the United Nations' Convention to Eliminate All Forms of Discrimination Against Women (CEDAW) as well as the Children's Rights Convention (CRC). The CRC, which is the most recent of these treaties, calls on countries to bestow certain rights on children as well as to actively promote their health and well-being.

FGM directly contravenes several provisions of the CRC. Article 24(3) requires nations to take all appropriate measures to abolish traditional practices prejudicial to the health of children; Article 19 proscribes child abuse; Article 16 provides a child with the right to privacy; and Article 37 prohibits children from being subjected to torture or cruel, inhuman, or degrading treatment.

The African Charter on the Rights and Welfare of the Child, adopted by the Organization of African Unity in 1990, promotes gender equality among children. Governments that sign the Charter are required to take all appropriate measures to eliminate harmful social and cultural practices affecting children, including practices that are discriminatory on the basis of sex.

As a result of women's activism at the Second World Conference on Human Rights in Vienna in June 1993, traditional and cultural practices harmful to women were mentioned specifically as a violation of human rights. Another success for advocates of women's and children's rights was achieved at the International Conference on Population and Development (ICPD). The ICPD document "Program for Action" has 4 articles with specific mention of FGM as a violation of reproductive health and rights.

International human rights bodies should define FGM as a form of child abuse. However, the comparison between FGM and child abuse must not go too far. It is very important to differentiate between the motivations for FGM and those for child beating or sexual abuse. FGM is undertaken with the intention of "normalizing" a girl, to make her equal to her peer group, whereas child abuse isolates a child, and subjects her to the whims of an adult.

The United Nations Women's Convention contains a "Bill of Rights" for women which can also be applied to FGM. The Convention calls on governments to modify or abolish customs and practices which constitute discrimination against women, and to modify practices which are based on the idea of female inferiority or stereotyped roles for men and women.

National Law

It is clear that there must be legal action against FGM within affected countries. The question then becomes: at what point and what kind of action is appropriate? Although legislation may be effective toward the prevention of FGM in countries where only a small minority are practitioners (such as Western countries with African immigrants), the problem is altogether different in places where a majority follows the tradition. In these instances, the sociocultural nature of the act as well as practitioners' ignorance of its consequences point to the greater need for public information campaigns about the effect of the practice on children and counseling of families whenever possible. Clear policy declarations by government and professional bodies are essential to send a strong message of disapproval, but if the majority of the society is still convinced that FGM serves the common good, legal sanctions that incriminate practitioners and families may be counterproductive. Criminalization and regulations are only effective once a substantial body of public opinion has been raised against the practice.

In the African context, most anti-FGM legislation was passed by colonial governments who looked upon the indigenous culture with disdain. These laws were decidedly ineffective. Most countries have been independent for several decades now, and it is necessary to reassess the relationship between governments and their people on this issue.

Only a few other African countries have specific legislation against FGM. In 1994 Ghana passed a law which explicitly prohibits FGM. Sudan had a law on its books for many years, although it was omitted from the 1991 legal revisions, as were many other laws, making their current status unclear. Egypt has had a Ministry of Health decree from the 1970s, which prohibits the performance of female circumcision by trained health professionals. In 1994 a ministerial decree was issued which medicalizes the practice with the parent's consent. Kenya banned FGM in 1990. In 1991, a representative of the Côte d'Ivoire told the United Nations that existing provisions of the nation's criminal code could be used to prohibit FGM. In Burkina some circumcising midwives have been brought to court and found guilty based on the interpretation of existing laws.

Discussion must now begin on where to draw the line between parental rights over children and the state's obligation to protect children from harm. This debate has already begun, both in Africa and abroad. In some countries, such as the United Kingdom and France, FGM has already been criminalized. In the United Kingdom, anti-FGM legislation is supplemented by the Children's Act of 1989, which provides for investigation of suspected violations of the FGM prohibition, as well as for removal of a child from her home in extreme cases where there is no better way to protect the child. The Children's Act also enables the courts to prohibit parents from removing their child from the country to have the operation performed elsewhere.

In France, legal precedent has placed FGM within the provisions of the criminal code that prohibits violence against and mutilation of children. Both parents and practitioners have been convicted and sentenced under the laws, receiving suspended sentences in most cases. Government officials in Canada, Italy, and Australia have also said that existing legislation concerning assault or battery, violence against a person's physical integrity, mutilation, and child abuse are applicable to FGM. In the United States the congressional women's caucus with the leadership of congresswoman Patricia Scroeder is sponsoring a bill to criminalize FGM. It was introduced unsuccessfully in 1994 and reintroduced in February 1995. The fate of the bill is still unknown.

Although laws alone will not eradicate FGM, legal measures must be pursued in all countries at the appropriate time. Changes in the law are evidence of the extent of government commitment to dealing with the issue; these changes also legitimize the work of anti-FGM advocacy groups.

As legal action against FGM increases in all affected societies, it is of paramount importance that countries reject measures calling for partial eradication of FGM by encouraging lesser forms of clitoridectomy or ceremonial procedures. Experience has shown that such policies only legitimize and perpetuate genital operations. Although in reality the decline of FGM may occur in stages, and some groups or families may first resort to milder forms before totally stopping the practice, official policy should always call for complete rejection of all forms of genital mutilation. The international community, as well as health and legal professionals, should join national governments in sending an unequivocal message that FGM in any form is unacceptable.

Recommendations for Action

Actions to stop FGM can be taken on many levels. Actors include international organizations such as the United Nations, influential aid and development agencies, national governments dealing with indigenous or immigrant communities, professional bodies, grassroots women's and youth groups, and other community organizations. The following is a short list of the kinds of action that ought to be considered.

International Programs

Agencies concerned with public health should develop policy positions on FGM as a risk to the sexual, reproductive, and psychological health and well-being of girls and women. Programs dealing with women's and children's health and family planning should include information on the health, religious, and sociocultural arguments against FGM. Counseling guidelines must be developed for health personnel which would describe how to deal with different personal attitudes toward FGM and how to overcome resistance to change. Health personnel must receive technical training on the complications of circumcision and how to handle women during and after childbirth.

International human rights bodies and organizations must declare FGM to be violence against women and children and a violation of their rights. They should press for the explicit inclusion of FGM in international and regional conventions and treaties, and concerned governments must be persuaded to sign and act on them. Governments must then be monitored for compliance, and the results published in a clear and widely accessible format.

Organizations and programs dealing with women's economic development must also address FGM, since a primary reason for its continuation is women's economic powerlessness. These agencies must earmark funds for work on FGM to ensure a satisfactory level of commitment and professional competence.

Professional Associations

Doctors', nurses', and midwives' professional associations must take clear positions against FGM and pass regulations prohibiting their members from providing it. They should communicate their policies clearly and unequivocally to their members, including the penalties that will be imposed on those who break the regulations. In countries where FGM is practiced by an immigrant minority, penalties on practitioners should be harsher (permanent withdrawal of license or imprisonment, for example) than in countries where the practice is pervasive (temporary withdrawal of license and wide public condemnation). The scarcity of trained health personnel in developing countries must be considered when thinking about penalties.

Professional legal associations at the international, regional, and national levels must have clear policy statements against FGM as a human rights violation. At the national level, these professional bodies must study possibilities of anti-FGM legislation, based on their understanding of specific laws and the legal strategy that would be most effective in each country. Successful legal and regulatory undertakings must be widely publicized to motivate other countries.

National or Community Programs

Programs may be broken down according to the social group they address, the type of activity undertaken and the agency or organization involved.

Constituencies or Social Groups

Everyone can and should be concerned with FGM: actions can be directed at or by women, men, youths, children, the elderly, midwives, teachers, media personnel, artists, singers, writers, actors. Certain programs, obviously, should be directed to the community as a whole.

Activities

Media approaches are central to an effective anti-FGM program. These would include information and discussion programs, plays, films, puppet shows, storytelling, posters, and radio and television campaigns. Artistic and literary competitions could also be used.

Programs should also be educational, utilizing both school curricula and training materials for teachers, counselors and youth group leaders.

Research activities would include developing reliable information on prevalence rates, the sexual and psychological effects of FGM, social attitudes, the potential of different constituencies for change, and effective messages and actions.

Agencies to undertake activities

These may be government institutions or non-governmental agencies, depending upon their existing areas of strength in each country. Departments of health, education, information, social affairs, and women's affairs should be involved. Health centers and clinics which serve women and children should be included, as should community organizers and social leaders.

The overriding consideration for all activities is that they be guided by the knowledge and wisdom of individuals from the communities involved, with special attention paid to the concerns of women. Unguided or patronizing interference from outsiders can create a backlash in favor of FGM, as has happened in the past.

Finally, it is important to emphasize that FGM is a part of a persistent global situation where women remain powerless because they lack access to resources, jobs, and education, and where women's bodies are controlled by a male-dominated social ideology. A global action against FGM cannot undertake to abolish this one violation of women's rights without placing it firmly within the context of efforts to address the social and economic injustice women face the world over. If women are to be considered as equal and responsible members of society, no aspect of their physical, psychological, or sexual integrity can be compromised.

Bibliography and Suggested Reading

—A'Haleem, Asma M. "Claiming Our Bodies and Our Rights: Exploring Female Circumcision as an Act of Violence." *Freedom From Violence*, Margaret Schuler, editor. OEF International, 1992. Available from United Nations/UNIFEM.

—Abdalla, Raqiya H.D. *Sisters in Affliction: Circumcision and Infibulation of Women in Africa*. London: Zed Books, 1982.

—An-Na'im, Abdullahi. *Toward an Islamic Reformation: Civil Liberties, Human Rights, and International Law*. Syracuse University Press, 1990.

—Assaad, Marie B. "Female Circumcision in Egypt: Social Implications, Current Research, and Prospects for Change." *Studies in Family Planning*, 11:1, January 1980.

—Balk, Deborah; Williams, Lindy; and Khadr, Zeinab. "Female Genital Mutilation in the Sudan: Demographic Correlates, 'Causes', and Consequences." Paper presented at the Population Association of America Annual Meeting, 1993.

—Dorkenoo, Efua. *Cutting the Rose: Female Genital Mutilation — The Practice and its Prevention*. Minority Rights Publication, 1994.

—El Dareer, Asma. *Woman, Why Do You Weep?* London: Zed Books, 1982.

—El Saadawi, Nawal. *Hidden Face of Eve: Women in the Arab World*. London: Zed Books, 1980.

—Gevins, A. "Tackling Tradition: African Women Speak Out Against Female Circumcision." *Third World, Second Sex*, compiled by Miranda Davis. London: Zed Books, 1987.

—Hosken, Fran. *The Hosken Report*. Fourth Edition. Lexington, MA. WIN NEWS, 1993.

—Koso-Thomas, Olayinka. *The Circumcision of Women: A Strategy for Eradication*. London: Zed Books, 1992.

—Lowry, Thomas et al. *The Clitoris*. St. Louis, MO: Warren Green, 1976.

—Skramstad, Heidi. *The Fluid Meanings of Female Circumcision in a Multiethnic Context in Gambia*. DERAP, Chr. Michelsen Institute, 1990.

—Somali Women's Democratic Organization. *Female Circumcision: Strategies to Bring about Change*. Proceedings of the International Seminar on Female Circumcision. 13–16 June 1988.

—Thiam, Awa. *Black Sisters Speak Out: Feminism and Oppression in Black Africa*. London: Pluto Press, 1986.

—Toubia, Nahid. "The Social and Political Implications of Female Circumcision: The Case of the Sudan." *Women and the Family in the Middle East*. E. Fernea, editor. Texas University Press, 1985.

—Toubia, Nahid. *Women of the Arab World*. London: Zed Press, 1988.

—*Traditional Practices Affecting the Health of Women and Children*. Report on a seminar, Khartoum, 10–15 February. WHO/EMRO Technical Publications, No. 2. 1979.

—Warzazi, Halima E. "Report of the United Nations Seminar on Traditional Practices Affecting the Health of Women and Children." Economic and Social Council, 5 July 1991.

About the Author

Nahid Toubia was born in Khartoum in 1951, and attended medical school in Egypt. In 1981 she became a fellow of the Royal College of Surgeons in England and the first woman surgeon in Sudan. She served as the head of the Pediatric Surgery department at Khartoum teaching hospital for many years. Recently, she worked for four years as an Associate for Women's Reproductive Health at the Population Council in New York City. She is currently an Associate Professor at Columbia University School of Public Health and Director of RAINBO. She is also a member of several scientific and technical advisory committees of the World Health Organization, UNICEF and UNDP and Vice-Chair of the advisory committee of the Women's Rights Watch Project of Human Rights Watch where she serves on the Board of Directors. She publishes widely on issues of reproductive health, women's rights, and gender inequality particularly in Africa and the Middle East.

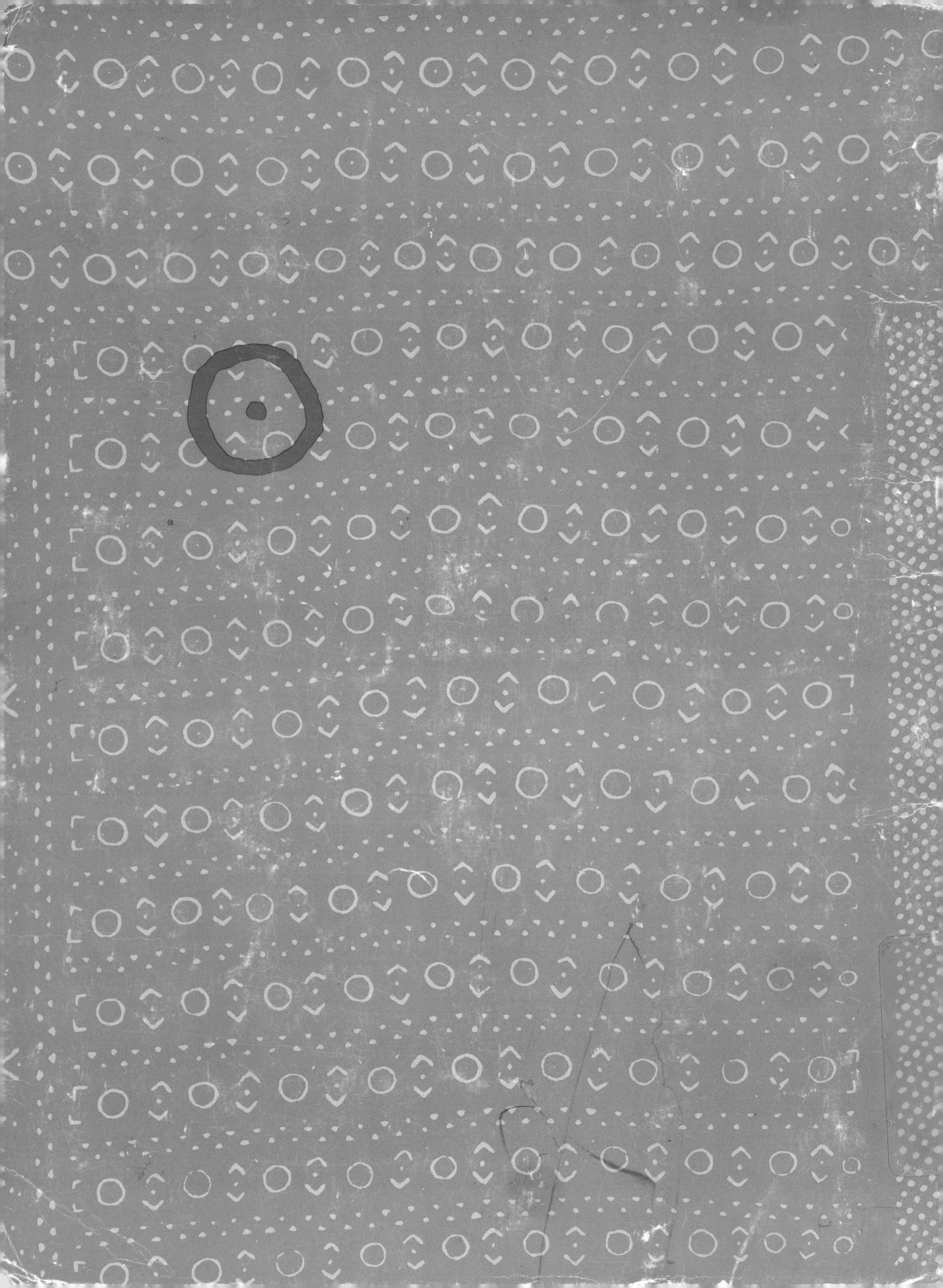